Pelvic Awakening

Pelvic Awakening

A Path to Reclaiming Power and

Vitality through Womb Connection

BETHANY WILDE

Published by Radiant Center Press

Copyright © 2025 Bethany Wilde

All rights reserved. No part of this book may be reproduced or used in any manner without written permission of the copyright owner except for the use of quotations in a book review.

The information provided in this book is designed to provide helpful information on the subjects discussed. This book is not meant to be used, nor should it be used, to diagnose or treat any medical condition. You are advised to seek the services of a healthcare professional regarding matters relating to your health. The author is not liable for any damages or negative consequences from any treatment, action, application, or preparation to any person reading or following the information in this book.

Back Author Photo: Samantha D'Anna

Cover art by Chelsea Skye. © 2020 Chelsea Skye. All Rights Reserved.

Hardcover Print ISBN: 978-1-7362261-3-1

Second Edition, September 2025

First Edition, January 2021

For my daughters

To the women who will read this book

Thank you for being here.

for arriving with an open heart and mind.

Let's begin by calling in your grandmothers to be with you.

Feel their great love moving through you.

Women are the lifeblood of families, of communities.

This is our time of awakening.

Women gathering in sisterhood,

healing, birthing in power,

remembering themselves as living expressions of Creation itself.

Listen within, and the way is revealed.

Contents

Introduction · 1

1. Our Matriarchal Roots

Page 15

2. Physical Female Anatomy

Page 31

3. Energetic Anatomy

Page 63

4. Cyclical Wisdom

Page 89

5. Clearing and Repatterning

Page 111

6. Practices for Pelvic Awakening

Page 137

7. Fertility and Pregnancy

Page 189

8. Postpartum and Motherhood

Page 211

9. Integration

Page 239

Share the Medicine · 247

Acknowledgements · 249

Citations · 251

Resources · 257

Pelvic Awakening Bonus · 261

About the Author · 263

Introduction

And she became her own temple, harboring the holiest of holies within her own womb

THE MADONNA SECRET

It was an exceptionally warm early spring day in the high desert of Central Oregon. Much of the snow had melted, opening the season to easier hiking after the long, frigid winter, when the wilderness felt off-limits by foot unless you had snowshoes. I moved slowly as I was still feeling the nausea and fatigue of early pregnancy. The hiking path surrounded a volcanic crater lake, which radiated a shade of blue that always left me in awe.

I walked around the lake near mountain hemlock trees and reedy marshes, obsidian shards scattered across the ground. This land was sacred to me; I had had many moments of quiet reflection and peace here. I reveled in these moments alone while dreaming of carrying my future child against my chest in this beloved place.

As I walked along the path deep in thought, I was abruptly brought into the present moment. Monarch butterflies appeared in small groups, then fully surrounded me in large numbers. My hand instinctively moved to my growing belly, and I closed my eyes and smiled, feeling a moment of grace.

Mirrored in the butterfly is the female pelvis, which I have dedicated years of study and devotion to in my work as a women's health bodyworker. Pregnancy had created a deeper sense of embodiment, and at that moment, I found a connection point.

A woman's pelvic bowl and the butterfly share so many traits, from the same sacred geometrical shape to the qualities both have as centers of transformation. I felt a deep interconnectedness to the natural world through the life passage I was walking. This alchemy was an ancient template passed throughout time.

Pelvic Connection

It's from this place of sacred embodiment that this journey begins. This book is a guide to knowing your pelvic bowl as your center, a place of power, intuition, and joy. It's a path of awakening.

There are many practical ways to develop this connection so that you can begin to see your body as a sanctuary, a place of safety and even bliss.

Through embodiment practices and re-orienting how you approach yourself, you can work through the feelings and memories that live here. Ultimately, this clears the way to experience a sense of groundedness and peace that is your birthright.

The pelvic bowl is the full landscape of the female pelvis—bones, muscles and soft tissues, reproductive organs, nerves, and the subtle energetic layers that live there.

I use various terms to describe the female body, anatomical and spiritual—pelvis, vagina, womb, *yoni*. *Yoni* is an Indian Sanskrit term interpreted to mean source or womb, and it also refers to a woman's sexual organs, such as her vagina and vulva. The Rigveda, the oldest known spiritual text in the world, refers to the *yoni* as the source and birthplace of life, a symbol of the feminine regenerative power of the universe [1]. I like using this term as it carries a reverence that's often absent in English when speaking of the female body.

Words are powerful; they change our consciousness, and the origin of them matters. When you speak of your body in appreciation, it's something you begin to feel within yourself.

Modern Womanhood

We live in a world that's governed by the rhythms of men. This looks like working year-round, with little or no space carved out for menstruation, pregnancy, or postpartum. A workday that doesn't align with children's school schedules. Men have daily hormonal peaks and lows like the sun, while women have monthly lunar rhythms and longer periods that require rest, such as the childbearing year.

This book explores the female body and energy system with a particular focus on the pelvic area. My approach draws from ancient traditions and modern experience, both research and years of hands-on work with women. Though everyone is unique, there are common energies that weave each woman together, rooted in the same design of the body.

My perspective explores the female experience that aligns with the true wisdom of the body. Although I appreciate traditional frameworks such as the concept of yin/yang, I am wary of modern "divine masculine and feminine" polarity teachings that reinforce limiting and harmful gender roles. This book invites reflection on an expansive, wild feminine, one that lives beyond stereotype. As you deepen your embodied connection to the feminine, you begin to feel who you really are.

Throughout the book, I speak more about these energetic principles that shape women, based on what I've seen in myself and witnessed in others. This is also informed by wisdom gathered across cultures, some of which you'll read about in Chapter 1. My hope is that you see these descriptions as expansive and illuminating possibilities, and that they help you feel the honor of embodying the feminine.

Beyond universal energetic patterns, embodiment is deeply personal. It's worth exploring what it means for *you* to be a woman and discover who you are at a soul-level, beyond what you've learned or inherited from your family, friends, and culture.

There are many moments in which to discover the treasures that lie within your body. It's often during important initiatory times (puberty, menstruation, pregnancy, birth, loss, postpartum, and menopause) that you can discover what you're made of, and begin to know yourself in deeper, *more real* ways.

If you've been pregnant, you've experienced an innate aspect of the feminine and felt its depth and power in your own body. Another potent time of connection to your female nature is during each month as you bleed, if you're in that phase of your life.

Modern women are in a unique time in history, one with abundant possibilities. When you come to a place of appreciation with your body and heal instinct injuries (the fractures in your inner knowing), you can return to wholeness. You can shift the culture toward something that's rooted in what truly nourishes life. Reclaiming this sense of power and wholeness through my womb is what led me to this work.

My Path to This Work

For much of my adult life, I've been drawn to women's work and wellness. I studied Somatic (body-based) Psychology in college, creating my own course of study about how trauma is stored in the body, and gentle, holistic ways to find resolution and healing. I also studied the shamanic and feminine roots of yoga and took an interest in ancient egalitarian, goddess-worshipping cultures.

A few years after graduating from college, I attended massage school intending to practice abdominal and uterine massage, pelvic floor bodywork, as well as fertility, pregnancy, and postnatal massage. After my initial massage training, I attended many specialized training workshops, read numerous books, and studied privately with mentors. I felt that through my connection to my womb and pelvic area, I encountered my deepest healing and sense of self. I knew I wasn't alone in feeling drawn to uncover what lay here.

I saw the lack of holistic and trauma-informed approaches to bodywork in this area and wanted to understand more and work with women in this way.

At the time, there weren't many people doing this work, and I had to search high and low for mentorship and training courses. I read obstetric and physical therapy textbooks that taught me extensive anatomy and real healing techniques. I gathered up everything I had learned and then began to sit with women and learn from them.

After having my first unassisted pregnancy and birth, I experienced a heightened sensitivity that evolved my work with women. I felt rooted in an instinctual knowing and naturally moved into more energetic work. I received imagery and felt ancestors and spirits when contacting the holy space of the womb. I began to work intuitively in more than just a physical way, gaining an understanding that this area was an opening to something beyond her, to something truly divine.

Then four years later, I had another healing unassisted birth, and my work evolved again. To give more time and energy to my children, I shifted to writing and medicine-making, and less in-person, hands-on work. This fulfilled my desire to share my thoughts and healing prescriptions with women in different ways.

As I write and edit this revised and updated second edition, I reflect on how I've been humbled by the deep and transformative spaces I've held with women, who have arrived with open minds and hearts. I've witnessed women's pregnancy journeys, from the sacred space of preconception to the often-dark places that women can go in their postpartum time. I've listened to the stories of women who held tragic and painful memories within their womb. Whose bodies tell the story of a culture and people who don't honor things that are life-giving. I've heard the grief of women as they reach the end of their bleeding years, making meaning from those years and gathering up their power. Pain, pleasure, numbness, blood mysteries, ancestors, and spirit babies. We hold so much.

I've learned from each woman I've spent time with. It's been the deepest honor to be invited in.

An Invitation

Within this book, you're invited to walk a self-guided journey. To spiral deep within the core of your physical being and energetic heart. To center your awareness within your holy pelvic bowl and discover what lives here. To clear what's holding you back and awaken who you really are.

I created this book to pass on what I've learned and witnessed, so that each woman can find the freedom that comes from a vibrant body, flowing with life force. It's my great joy to support women in their path to healing and reclamation.

This book is for any woman, but especially those who sense both wounds and gifts are waiting to be uncovered here.

It's for women healing from trauma who are ready to access a new, embodied layer of their truth.

For the women yearning to awaken sensation, increase pleasure, nourish their creative lives, and feel safe in their bodies.

Whether you're walking a healing path, preparing for conception, or simply longing to uncover the wisdom of your womb, this book is for you.

A Note Before You Begin

Before you dive in, take a breath. This isn't another book of exercises or things to do, but an invitation to return to yourself.

If you're here, it may be because something feels off. Perhaps your body has guided you to bring attention to your womb space. You may have thought:

"There's so much held there."

"There's pain, and it's not just physical."

"I have painful periods or womb issues, and nothing has helped."

"This area feels numb, or like I'm not connected to that part of me."

"It's the part of my body I avoid."

The core message of this book is that you can trust yourself. Your body speaks in subtle promptings and whispers, and sometimes loud symptoms. You are being called inward and you can let that guide you, without second guessing yourself.

This book offers a path: a collection of practices, insights, and stories to help you reconnect with your womb and your inherent power. Inside, you'll find tools for nourishment, energetic clearing, embodiment, and remembering. After reading, my hope is that you will feel more rooted in your body, supported with practices that nourish and heal. That you will feel more alive, grounded, and at ease in your everyday life.

Let this be your reminder: your body already knows the way. This book offers guidance, but your body holds the template to its radiance and inner truth.

If you're feeling overwhelmed, just take a moment of presence with yourself. Even a hand on your womb and a deep breath can bring subtle shifting. You can move through this book in order or let your intuition guide you.

If you'd like to start with a quick and simple internal shift, try the Womb-Heart Spiral meditation first on page 173. Let this entire book be a return to yourself, not another task to do. You don't need to do every practice to receive the medicine. You can return to this book again and again, each time uncovering a new layer of yourself.

And as you go through the pages, check in with yourself. Don't accept my words as your truth. Consider what feels true in your body and in your heart, and let that guide you.

Let's begin.

I

Our Matriarchal Roots

Remembering Our Lineage

Woman is by nature a shaman.

CHUKCHEE PROVERB

Across all lineages, if we go back far enough, we find a time when the Earth was a living mother. When the womb was honored. When the blood of women was seen as life-giving. These ways of seeing the world, and the cultures they come from, are more alike than they are different.

We live within a time of imbalance, where nearly all things life-affirming and holy are seen as shameful or unimportant. Where the sacred feminine is diminished.

We know, deep within us, that other ways of life once existed. Riane Eisler, historian and author of *The Chalice and the Blade*, explores a beautiful hidden history. Across cultures and time, ancient societies valued balance, partnership, and held a deep reverence for life.

But the world we live in today is different. Instead of equality and connection, we live within what Eisler calls a dominator model: a system where "fear and force maintain rigid understandings of power and superiority in a hierarchical structure" [1].

These earlier partnership-oriented cultures thrived long before and even after the beginning of agriculture, which is often seen as a turning point. Around 10,000 years ago, as people began to settle, there was a gradual shift in worldview. Nomadic people who once lived in harmony with the Earth and its cycles began to move into ways of control and ownership. First, this was over land and animals, then eventually over women. This transition didn't happen all at once. Some cultures moved towards hierarchy and control, while others continued to live in balance for much longer.

Archaeologist Marija Gimbutas and scholars like Eisler studied ancient figurines, art, and fragments of early writing. Through this work, they uncovered evidence of societies that honored the feminine and organized life around cycles of nature, fertility, and community well-being. What emerged was a womb-centered cosmology, a way of understanding the universe that placed the feminine and the cycles of life at the center.

As described in the book *Womb Awakening*, "Sexual symbology was inseparable from religious symbology. Sex was sacred. Death, birth, rebirth, personal transformation, shamanic journey, spiritual power, and the alchemical act of merging into oneness consciousness with another all happened through the portal of the yoni-womb."

Over 90% of ancient figurines found around the world are of women. They're shown pregnant, birthing, bleeding, dancing—with open *yonis* and wide hips, bodies seen as sacred vessels of life. Spirals, circles, and downward-pointing triangles often appear within them. In Paleolithic cave art, red ochre paint, the color of blood and birth, is found again and again, symbolizing the life-giving power of the womb [2].

When you look at the art and artifacts of the past, it becomes clear that the female form was centered and revered. Creation myths from around the world echo the same stories of the Great Mother, the cosmic womb from which all life is born.

Women's bodies, and all the fluids that emerge from them, were seen as sacred. In the book *Blood Politics: Race, Culture, and Identity in the Cherokee Nation of Oklahoma*, Circe Dawn Sturm writes that among the Cherokee, menstrual blood was considered a source of profound feminine strength, a viewpoint seen across the world.

In this chapter, I journey through three lineages that are meaningful to me: Old Europe, Ancient India, and early Hebrew traditions. Each carried a womb-centered view of the world and ways of living rooted in harmony with nature and the creative force of life.

Losing touch with these ancestral ways has contributed to the widespread disconnection and unspoken grief that so many women feel today. Let these symbols and stories awaken something deep inside of you that already knows what is sacred and meaningful.

Learning about these cultures has changed my life and how I move through the world. My hope is that it will offer you the same kind of expansion and remembering.

When the Goddess was Everywhere

In ancient Europe, the Goddess was at the heart of their ways of life. These early civilizations, flourishing around 7000–3000 BCE, left behind thousands of female figurines, ceremonial shrines, and symbols celebrating women, the womb, and nature.

In Çatalhöyük, the earliest intact Goddess site in the world (7000 BCE), archaeologists uncovered figurines of women in meditation, dance, and birthing positions. James Mellart, the site's original excavator, observed that statues of female deities far outnumbered male ones, and in some places, only female figures were found. [3]

The body of a woman wasn't separate from the divine. It *was* the divine. Feminist scholar Vicki Noble writes: "If these images had been found in India or Tibet, they would automatically be taken as sacred icons of a female deity. In the West, these implications are often dismissed or ignored" [4].

Many early interpretations by male archaeologists downplayed the spiritual significance of the female form, viewing these artifacts as fertility symbols rather than reflections of a living, sacred worldview.

Seated Mother Goddess figurine from Çatalhöyük. Source: Wikimedia Commons.

"Matriarchal" doesn't mean the opposite of patriarchy. These were not female-dominated societies rooted in hierarchy, but rather ones centered in partnership. Many of these cultures were peaceful, with no clear evidence of war [5]. Of course, no culture is perfect, but they offer a glimpse of societies who oriented toward connection, not control.

In Ancient Europe's womb-centered worldview, the Goddess was represented as maiden, mother, and crone. These were living archetypes reflected in seasonal rituals, agricultural ceremonies, and rites of passage.

Marija Gimbutas noted how tombs, shrines, and temples were built as symbolic wombs and painted red. These were places where initiates or those who died would enter to be spiritually "reborn" from the body of the Earth mother.

Life was seen as a cyclical process of birth, death, and rebirth. Unlike later traditions that divided the sacred into good and evil and viewed time as linear, Neolithic spirituality embraced wholeness and the spiral nature of life.

Remembering these Goddess-centered civilizations offers powerful medicine. These societies tell us that patriarchy, with its systems of conquering, and devaluing the feminine, isn't the original blueprint for human life.

The ancient cultures of Europe remind us that the female body is sacred. The rhythms of the Earth and the seasons of the womb were once seen as holy mirrors of each other. Both God and Goddess were known alongside each other.

These ways aren't lost. You can always weave this remembering back into your life.

Shakti: The Pulse of Ancient India

In ancient India, the divine feminine was the pulse of existence itself. *Shakti*, the dynamic creative force of the Universe, was seen to flow through all of life. Women were considered to be the embodiment of *Shakti's* creative power, living expressions of transformation and renewal.

Before the rise of patriarchal culture, the Indus Valley Civilization (3300–1900 BCE) and surrounding areas knew the feminine as a sacred energy. These cultures were organized around water and fertility. Figurines of women with wide hips and exposed *yonis* were found alongside sacred trees, decorated with serpents and symbols of cyclical renewal. These early societies appear to have been egalitarian, with life centered around the rhythms of agriculture, lunar cycles, and worship of the Great Mother [6].

Though the Indus Valley left behind written records that remain undeciphered, its symbols and figurines speak of a deep feminine presence, one that echoes through time. Later Tantric traditions carried forward some of these same threads: the honoring of *Shakti*, expressed through nature, sexuality, birth, and death.

In Tantra, the body wasn't seen as a hindrance to our spirituality, it was seen as *the* pathway to the divine.

Mother Goddess figurine from Indus Valley. Source: National Museum of India in New Delhi.

In Tantra, the *yoni* is seen as the gateway to *Shakti*, representing the source of all creation. Noble describes the "female blood roots" of yoga and shamanism, ancient practices in which women cultivated energy through two bodies: the physical and the energetic, visualized like a serpent interwoven with the body. The serpent has long been a feminine symbol of spiritual power, and is represented as *kundalini*, energy coiled at the base of the spine, awaiting activation. [10] This life force rises from the root to awaken each of the energy centers above.

In Tantric texts, the blood of a woman's *yoni* was considered magical, and used in rituals of healing, loving union, and spiritual transcendence [7].

Today, many pelvic healing practices draw inspiration from these Tantric traditions: seeing the womb as a center of power, the sacredness in our sexuality, and the body as a path to liberation.

When you dance, practice womb meditation, or reclaim *yoni* massage, you can return to the body as a holy temple. Within the center of you lies the very pulse of life.

Under the Sacred Trees: Remembering Asherah

The children gather wood, the fathers kindle fire, and the women knead dough, to make cakes for the queen of heaven.

JEREMIAH 7:18

This lineage is my own, through both my maternal and paternal lines. The Jewish people, like all peoples, carry the memory of the old wisdom ways.

For years, I had been drawn to ancient cultures that honored the feminine: to the goddesses of Old Europe, the female shamans and priestesses, the partnership-based worldviews I studied in college. But I realized I hadn't yet looked deeply into my own ancestral line. What threads of feminine wisdom might have once existed there, beneath the layers of history and suppression?

I didn't grow up religious, and I've never resonated with patriarchal frameworks. But when I traveled to Israel at age 23, something stirred in me. I wasn't expecting to feel so at home right away. Visiting Mary Magdalene's hometown and walking her same paths, standing among sacred ruins, sleeping under the vast sky in the Negev desert. It felt like I was surrounded by family wherever I went. The young people I met on the sandy banks of the Jordan River, who invited me to eat with them. The old woman I spoke to on the train up the Mediterranean coast to Haifa. There was a feeling of belonging that I hadn't experienced anywhere else before.

Since then, I've searched for what lies beneath modern Judaism. Like most ancient traditions, early Hebrew spirituality once carried a story of feminine balance and a deep relationship with the cycles of life.

Before modern beliefs centered around one male god, the feminine aspect of the divine was its counterpart. One of the earliest Hebrew goddesses was Asherah, known as the Queen of Heaven. She was worshipped across the ancient near East as a mother goddess, connected to fertility, sexuality, and the abundance of life [8].

Asherah was deeply tied to nature. She was symbolized by trees and worshipped in sacred groves. These groves were places of prayer and fertility rituals, and where seasonal ceremonies were held. It's likely that priestesses tended these groves, and the tree was her living symbol: a bridge between worlds. Rooted deep in the earth, reaching into the heavens, this symbol echoes across cultures: the Kabbalah's Tree of Life, the chakra system, the great world tree mythologies.

Asphodel Long, in her research on the goddess in Judaism, writes that Asherah "embodied the whole female principle of life... and was revered as both tree and the source of life" [9].

Ancient figurines representing Asherah show women with hands cupped beneath their breasts, displaying the nourishment and abundance that comes from a woman's body. Many figurines of her image are considered to have been amulets that were used to promote fertility or provide protection during childbirth.

Asherah figurine. Source: Wikimedia Commons.

As the story has repeated across time, Asherah's memory was suppressed. Her altars were destroyed (2 Kings 23:6) and her worship was called sinful. Over time, the divine feminine was pushed aside.

And yet, her presence continues in the symbolism of the *Shekhinah* (the feminine presence of God in the mystical tradition of Kabbalah), in the Tree of Life, and deep in the hearts of the Jewish people. Somewhere deep within, we all know that without the feminine, something vital is lost.

When I speak the name Asherah, when I see her images, it's like a long-forgotten memory. My roots run through those sacred groves.

This hidden history is deeply encouraging. It tells us that patriarchy is not the origin of human society. That a civilization built on disconnection and domination isn't inevitable. For perhaps hundreds of thousands of years before, cultures flourished that honored the Earth and its rhythms. These societies understood that life was sacred, and that the womb held immense power.

Much of our past as modern humans, spanning at least 300,000 years, remains a mystery. It's likely that there have been countless cycles of tribal life and ways of being. But what we can gather from the traces left behind is that living in balance with the earth and one another was more common than anything else.

As you restore a kind of cellular memory, when you remember that the female body was once revered, that women's rhythms shaped ways of life, something begins to heal.

These old stories of Goddesses, womb temples, and priestesses live inside each of us. They give us symbols and stories that speak to what we know is sacred.

It's not about idealizing or recreating the past. You can use what touches you as a template to inspire your own life by these values. As you root yourself in an ancestral lineage of partnership, you play a part in creating a more aligned, loving world.

Let this chapter be an invitation to remember that the stories and the wisdom aren't lost. Be inspired by these cultures to look into your own lineage and its traditions. Find the names of your ancient mother goddesses. There is healing when you call them back into your heart and speak their names aloud.

Integration

Remembering matriarchal, womb-honoring cultures reshapes what we believe is possible. Rooting yourself in this ancestral context deepens healthy embodiment and shifts how you relate to your lineage, your body, and the meaning of feminine power by reclaiming it as sacred rather than shameful.

1. Where does your lineage originate from? Have you explored the pre-patriarchal or folk traditions of your ancestral line? (*Tip: ancestry.com is a great start, along with asking elders in your family for their stories*)
2. How have you felt about the cyclical rhythms of your body, and your menstrual cycle each month? After reading this chapter, do you feel anything has changed?

2

Physical Female Anatomy

Mapping the Terrain of the Sacred Female Pelvis

The body is not an obstacle to the spiritual path.

It is the path.

KṢEMARĀJA

Before getting to the physical practices, let's begin by attuning to the terrain of your body. Understanding your anatomy deepens a connection with your physical form and the magic held within. Knowing the internal landscape is the starting point to pelvic awakening. Having this mental map is empowering, helping to visualize and feel the places within, ultimately shifting into feeling good in your body.

This chapter offers an overview of the anatomy of the pelvic bowl, and this foundation is meant to orient you before moving into energetic anatomy as well as the pelvic care practices. For those wanting to deepen their anatomical studies, you'll find a list of recommended books in the Resources section.

The Sacred Pelvic Bowl

I first heard the term "pelvic bowl" after training with Tami Kent, a women's physical therapist and author of *Wild Feminine: Finding Power, Spirit & Joy in the Female Body*. Tami is the creator of Holistic Pelvic Care, a physical and energetic modality that supports internal pelvic floor healing.

If you observe the shape of the pelvis, it's undeniably the shape of a bowl. Vessels have a long association with women, not only for their connection to water, nourishment, and traditional women's work, but for their symbolic quality of receiving. Bowls are made by the worn, wise hands of women to nourish. Women fill them and pour life-giving substances into the mouths of their children, the community, and the Earth itself. This is the domain of women.

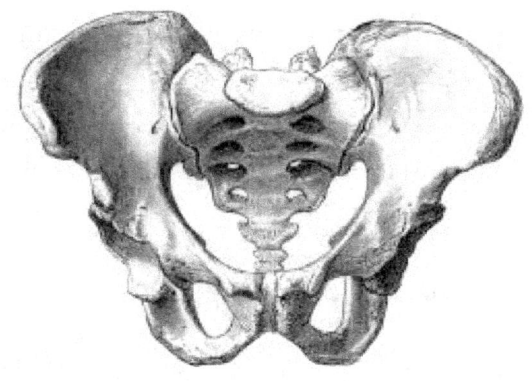

Image of the female pelvis. Source: Wikimedia Commons.

When I see the female pelvis, I see all of this. I see the singing bowl, resonating harmony and blessings through its space. I see a vessel that supports the internal organs, holding and protecting life. I see a child growing, nourished within the womb. I invite you to begin visualizing your pelvis in this way too; to see your body as a living temple.

In the introduction, I shared a personal moment with butterflies, a symbolic experience that has continued to echo in my work. In the image of the pelvis, you can see the shape of the butterfly (see the cover art of this book). And its transformation is an ancient archetype that lives in our bones. It speaks of growth, death, and rebirth, and it's mirrored in the journey of the female body. When you see your pelvic bowl as a matrix of transformation, you recognize that possibility is your very nature.

The pelvis isn't just the energetic root of the feminine spirit, it's also the structural foundation of the body. It houses vital organs and many layers of soft tissue that support everything from below.

The female pelvis differs from the male pelvis in several ways: it's typically wider and rounder, with a shorter and wider sacrum. These are nature's way of supporting pregnancy and the opening required for birth. In fact, the differences between the male and female pelvis are so distinct that the pelvis is what archaeologists use to determine whether a skeleton belongs to a male or female.

During labor, the soft tissues and ligaments of the pelvis soften and stretch, allowing the bones to shift and widen, and then afterward, they come back together.

In the next section, I'll guide you through some of the major pelvic landmarks so you can better visualize this structure within yourself. I encourage you to feel for these places in your own body as you go along.

Anatomical Landmarks of the Pelvis

The pelvis is your center. These bones are the heaviest and densest in the body, made for strength and endurance. The female pelvis is uniquely designed to hold life and expand when needed.

It's helpful to start with the structure and its bony landmarks. These are physical features you can feel from the outside that help orient you to your own internal landscape. They are attachment points for muscles, ligaments, and tendons.

The pelvis is made up of two hip bones (that includes 3 fused bones: the ilium, ischium, and pubis). At the back, the sacrum connects the two sides, with the tailbone (coccyx) extending downward. These bones join at the pubic symphysis in the front and the sacroiliac (SI) joints at the back on either side of the sacrum.

Both joints are supported by strong ligaments that allow typically limited movement, in order to provide stability.

You can refer to the diagram as you go along, mapping these structures within your own body.

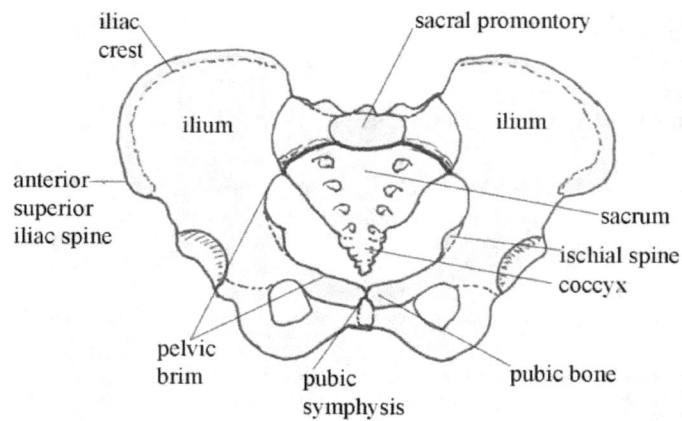

Bones of the female pelvis. Source: open.edu

Pubic Bone and Pubic Symphysis

You can locate your pubic bone by feeling the hard ridge about 1–2 inches below where your pubic hair begins. Trace this ridge with your fingers. At the center, you'll feel a slight dip: this is the pubic symphysis, where the two sides of the pubic bone come together. This point marks the front of your pelvic bowl. During pregnancy, this area opens, and many women feel a distinct instability.

Sit Bones (Ischial Tuberosities)

You can probably recognize your sit bones when on a hard surface. They're the two bony points you feel underneath your glutes. These form the base of your pelvis, connecting you to the Earth and offering support from below.

Hip Bones (ASIS: Anterior Superior Iliac Spine)

You may be surprised by how high the bones of your pelvis reach. Place your hands on either side of your waist, just below your ribs, and slowly inch downward until you reach bone. These are your hip bones, the highest part of your pelvis. Now you can get a greater sense of how much space this sacred structure holds within you.

Sacrum and Tailbone (Coccyx)

The sacrum is the triangular bone at the base of the spine. Often, it's larger and takes up more space than you may imagine. The sacrum is an extension of the spine, but the vertebrae are fused to provide stability. The sacrum extends into the tailbone, which ideally would lie flat with a slight and natural curve to it, but many people have an exaggerated, curved tailbone from falls, trauma, or restrictions in their fascia. This is the back wall of your pelvic bowl. The sacroiliac (SI) joint is where the pelvis connects to the sacrum.

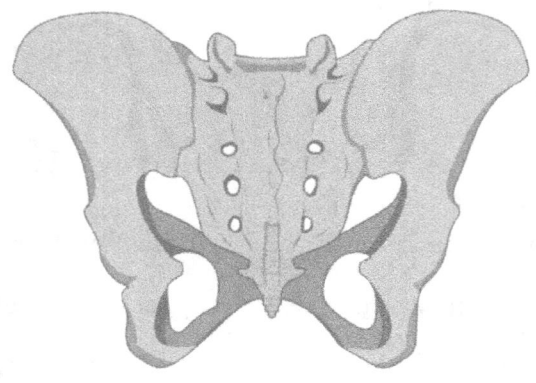

View of the female pelvis from behind, highlighting the sacrum, tailbone, and SI joints. Source: Wikimedia Commons.

The word sacrum means "sacred" in Latin, suggesting ancient interpretations of this bone as important in the cycle of life. In Pre-Hispanic Mesoamerican traditions and some Old-World cultures, the sacrum represented reincarnation and was considered a doorway between this world and the next [1].

You can see why this association began with people witnessing birth throughout the ages. During childbirth, the sacrum acts as a "door" so the child can pass through. Labor begins with a normal neutral position, then powerful hormones allow pelvic ligaments and muscles to move the sacrum and tailbone outward. You can picture this in the direction of how a dog door opens, but of course, more subtly.

The sacrum houses a rich network of nerves. Through openings (called the sacral foramen), these nerves travel to the organs and tissues within the pelvis. Many people carry tension or padding in this area from a sedentary lifestyle, past injuries, or emotional guarding. Massaging with castor oil and using castor oil packs can help soften this tissue and restore circulation throughout the pelvic bowl. See Chapter 6 for guidance with these practices.

The Uterus: Palace of Yin

The uterus, or womb, lies deep within the pelvis. In Taoist language, this organ is known by many names: *the palace of yin, the inner heart, the heavenly palace* [2]. These poetic names hint at the sacredness and mystery of this space.

The uterus is a hollow, muscular organ that contracts rhythmically throughout the month, especially during orgasm, menstruation, and birth. These contractions reflect the deep intelligence of the womb.

The uterus plays a key role in pregnancy, fertility, and the menstrual cycle. Each month, the inner uterine lining (endometrium) builds up and then releases if conception doesn't happen. If you do conceive, the fertilized egg implants within the thickened, blood-rich uterine lining and is nourished by it until the placenta takes over a couple of months later.

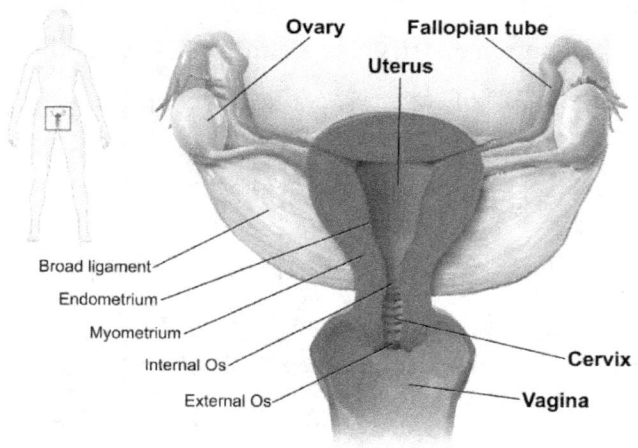

Image of the uterus, tubes, and ovaries. Source: Wikimedia Commons.

A simple way to locate your uterus is to place your hands together in an inverted triangle, mirroring the ancient Tantric symbol of the *yoni*. Where your middle fingers naturally rest is often the top of the uterus, while the spaces between your ring and pinky fingers are roughly where your ovaries reside.

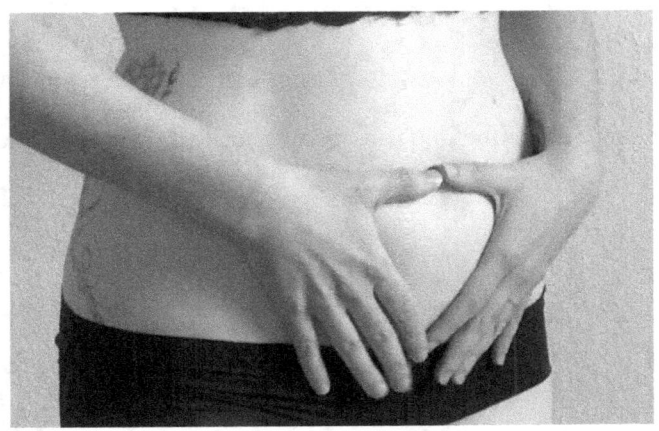

Photo illustrating how to locate your uterus. Source: Author.

From this position, you can also feel for the pubic bone (often just below your middle fingers) and at the center, the point where the two bones meet: the pubic symphysis. Below the pubic bone lies the bladder and then behind that is your uterus. If it's in an optimal position, and you are not pregnant or menstruating, you won't be able to feel it.

In the following images, you can see how the bladder, uterus, and rectum are positioned within the pelvic bowl. The uterus sits behind the bladder and in front of the rectum, all with many layers of muscle, fat, and fascia surrounding. This is why you typically can't feel the uterus directly unless it's significantly out of alignment or you're pregnant.

The uterus plays a key role in pelvic alignment along with all other organs. It acts as a placeholder, helping to support positioning of the bladder and rectum, and the abdominal organs above it.

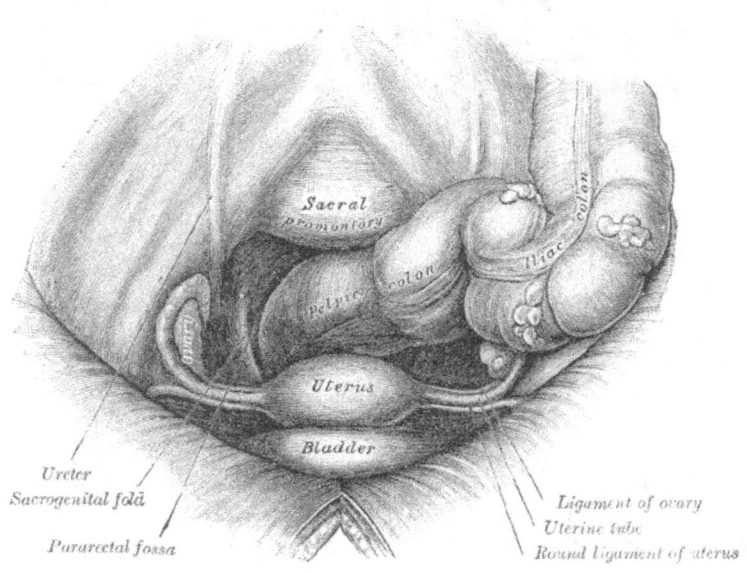

View from above, where the bladder is at the front of the body. Source: Gray's Anatomy.

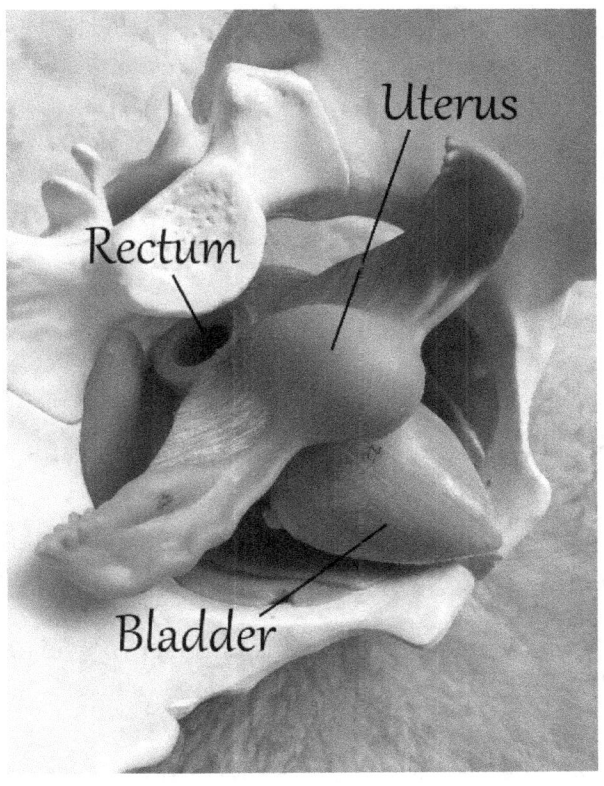

View from above. The pubic bone on the front is on the right side of the photo, and the sacrum is on the left side Source: Author.

When you're not pregnant, the uterus weighs about one ounce. At the beginning of your menstrual cycle, when it begins to shed the lining it has built up all month, it can weigh around two to three ounces. This often accounts for the full, heavy feeling many women experience during their bleed. And after carrying a child, it'll remain slightly larger than in a woman who has never been pregnant [3].

Uterine Alignment

The uterus is held in alignment by several ligaments. This doesn't mean "held in place"; this organ has a natural mobility. When the bladder is full, the uterus may shift backward. When the rectum is full, it may tip forward.

This natural movement is normal, but sometimes this mobility can lead to shifts in alignment. This can happen when ligaments change length (such as during pregnancy), connective tissue becomes weaker (like after injury), or when excessive downward pressure occurs (such as with belly breathing).

The image below shows one of the key uterine supports, the broad ligament, and a few more that anchor the uterus and ovaries to surrounding structures. Everything in the body is connected and interrelated.

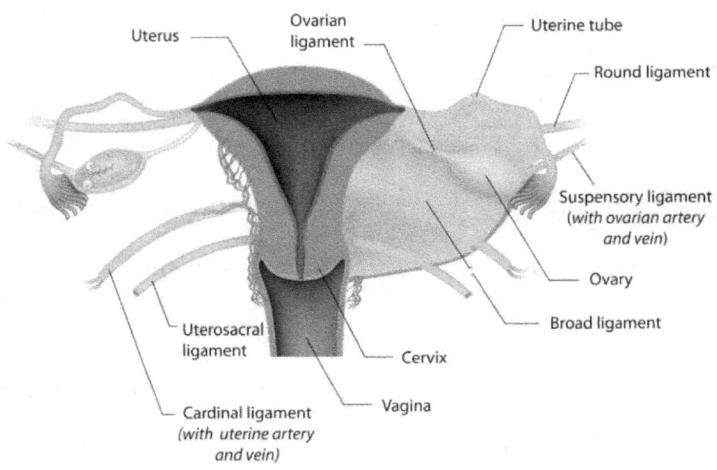

View of the key uterine ligaments. Source: Alila Medical Media.

Why does alignment matter? In a centered position, there's better circulation of blood and lymph for its optimal health. This can also support fertility, pregnancy, and birth. That said, many women have "non-optimal" positioned uteri and experience no issues at all. The most common variations in positioning include retroflexed or retroverted (tilted back toward the rectum, anteflexed or anteverted (tipped more forward onto the bladder), and/or leaning toward the left or right.

Some common contributors to the womb coming out of alignment include pregnancy experiences, running on hard surfaces, falls, or tailbone/sacral injuries. Other causes include a sedentary lifestyle, frequently wearing heeled shoes, and even emotional armoring.

Of course, there may be many more reasons, just as with any other part of the body that moves out of alignment. The good news is that you don't need to get overly technical or stressed about the exact position. Simply intuitively massaging your abdomen and womb increases circulation and restores harmony in numerous ways. This enables your body to come into its *own* optimal alignment. You can see Chapter 6 for a guided massage practice.

The Ovaries: Hidden Treasures

Roughly the size of a walnut, the ovaries produce the hormones that regulate your menstrual cycle and support reproduction. They make and release eggs, typically one per cycle, for all your fertile years.

Each ovary has thousands of ovarian follicles, which are sacs that hold immature eggs. During the follicular phase, the ovaries produce follicle-stimulating hormone (FSH) that matures them. Then, they release luteinizing hormone (LH) that triggers the release of an egg during ovulation. The ovaries also produce estrogen and progesterone, which affect your cycle, mood, and a potential pregnancy.

For those in the pre-conception phase, supporting the health of your eggs is essential. The three months leading up to conception are especially impactful—everything you do during that time directly affects egg quality [4].

All the eggs in your body were already present when you were in your mother's womb. That means the building blocks of you once lived inside your mother, and inside her mother. Your ovaries carry the physical encoding of DNA and the energetic imprint of your maternal line.

In Taoism, ovaries are known as the Hidden Treasures. They are seen as reservoirs of powerful, creative energy. Each ovary contains thousands of eggs, each of them carrying the potential to create an entire human. When you focus on womb connection and healing, don't forget the ovaries. These organs house a powerful creative fire, with transformative energy.

For decades, science has taught that women are born with all the eggs they will ever have and that they diminish over time, never to be replenished. It's said girls begin puberty with around 300,000 eggs and then are down to about 25,000 by age 40 [5].

But in recent years, researchers discovered ovarian stem cells in adult mice, which are cells that were able to produce new eggs. In follow-up studies, these eggs even led to the birth of viable offspring [6].

While this hasn't yet been confirmed in humans as of 2025, it's a groundbreaking shift in our understanding of female biology. It opens exciting possibilities for how we understand the regenerative nature of the ovaries.

You can access this powerful creative energy even outside of fertility. These organs hold a vital life force that can be directed into other areas of expression, creation, and vision. After menopause, women can find the energy within their ovaries even more potent.

A simple practice: place your hands over each ovary, one at a time. Feel into the energy there. Massage the area very gently and intuitively. Do you notice different energies within each side? Let this be a moment to reconnect and envision your dreams.

The Cervix: A Portal

Most women don't think much about the cervix or where it is until they want to get pregnant. The quality of the fluids that emerge here, the feel, and the position all give important information as to your current state of fertility.

The cervix is technically the lower portion of the uterus (and can be felt at the deepest place in the vagina), but unlike its smooth muscular walls, the cervix is made of dense connective tissue. It's also constantly changing. During menstruation, it tends to be lower, firmer, and slightly open, allowing blood to pass through. During ovulation, it rises, softens, and becomes wetter and more open to allow fertile cervical fluid to pass. This fluid helps sperm survive and travel its way towards an egg.

Understanding the monthly changes in your cervix connects you more deeply with your body and fertility. Whether you're trying to conceive or avoid pregnancy, this awareness can offer a non-hormonal form of birth control. If you're curious to explore more, I recommend *Taking Charge of Your Fertility* by Toni Weschler.

The cervix is also a doorway to life, literally and energetically. During the liminal few days per month when you're fertile, your cervix opens to receive and create the alchemy for new life within you. And if conception occurs, this same opening becomes the gateway through which life enters the world.

In Taoist systems of genital reflexology as described by Mantak Chia [7], different zones inside the vagina are said to correspond with different organs and energy centers. The cervix is associated with the heart, a connection many women describe feeling through their own lived experience. Cervical orgasms often carry a distinct, heart-opening quality. For many, this type of connection is transcendent.

The Cervix-Oxytocin Connection

Tiny receptors in the cervical tissue communicate with your body to release oxytocin in response to various stimuli. Oxytocin, often called the "love hormone," is associated with bonding, pleasure, and a deep feeling of calm and connection.

This is one reason I love herbal pelvic steaming (a practice described in Chapter 6). When the warm steam touches the cervix, it activates these receptors, often triggering the deeply relaxed feeling many women experience afterward.

Interestingly, the highest concentration of oxytocin receptors occurs during the luteal phase (after ovulation, and before a woman's period), and the absolute peak in a woman's life happens at the end of pregnancy [8].

With such a potent web of connections, the cervix can act as a site of memory and emotional imprint, and a place where sensations, stories, and energetic experiences may be held. And for many women, it's also a place affected by modern medical procedures and interventions, which can create scar tissue or loss of sensation over time.

Cervical Scar Tissue

If you've ever had a procedure involving your cervix, you may have some scar tissue in that area.

A scar is your body's natural response to injury, as it forms dense, fibrous tissue in place of the more elastic tissue that was originally there. Scar tissue is normal and generally goes through a remodeling process where it eventually returns to a healthy state again. In other parts of the body, like the shoulder, physical therapy begins right away to restore mobility after surgery.

But the cervix is different. It's internal, often numb, and typically not touched or tended to after procedures. When cervical scar tissue remains dense or spreads, it can decrease nerve supply, limit movement in surrounding fascia and muscle, and impact circulation, sensation, fertility, and birth outcomes.

It can be difficult to know if you have scar tissue or how much. Often, younger women tend to get more than older women, since they have a bigger scar response to injury or surgery.

Aviva Romm, MD, herbalist and midwife, has written about this phenomenon on her blog. She observed that many of her clients who had undergone common cervical procedures later struggled to dilate during labor, believed to be linked to the presence of scar tissue [9].

So, how do you know if you might have cervical scar tissue? It can result from a wide range of common procedures or experiences, including:

- IUD insertion or removal
- Cervical biopsies
- LEEP and LLETZ procedures
- Cryosurgery to the cervix
- D&C (dilation and curettage)

- Cervical tearing during childbirth
- Long term use of hormonal birth control (1 year or more)
- Previous cesarean birth
- Pelvic inflammatory disease
- Endometriosis
- Emotional armoring or trauma

If you think you may have scar tissue or simply want to reconnect with this area of your body after any of these experiences, you have options. You can work with a pelvic floor physical therapist or trained bodyworker who understands cervical care and scar tissue. These practitioners can offer bodywork and help you learn techniques to continue at home (see Resources).

You can also begin this work on your own. See Chapter 6 for guidance with pelvic floor massage and scar tissue healing.

Pelvic Floor Muscles

The pelvic floor muscles form the base of the pelvic bowl. They're layered, multidimensional, and often difficult to visualize at first.

A good place to begin is with multiple images of the pelvis and even a model if you're inspired. The bony landmarks of the pelvis (page 53) are the places where the pelvic floor muscles attach. You can imagine them like a hammock, spanning from front to back, providing structure and support for everything above: pelvic organs (uterus, ovaries, bladder, rectum), abdominal organs, and the connective tissue that holds it all together.

These muscles are typically divided into three layers, from the most surface level, middle, and the deepest layer.

These muscles hold a lot, so they need to be strong. But they also need to be supple and responsive, able to adapt to shifting internal conditions: your bladder and rectum filling and emptying, your uterus changing in size throughout your cycle or pregnancy, your vagina opening and then softening again.

Having an internal map is a helpful starting place for the deeper exploration of vaginal massage later in the book.

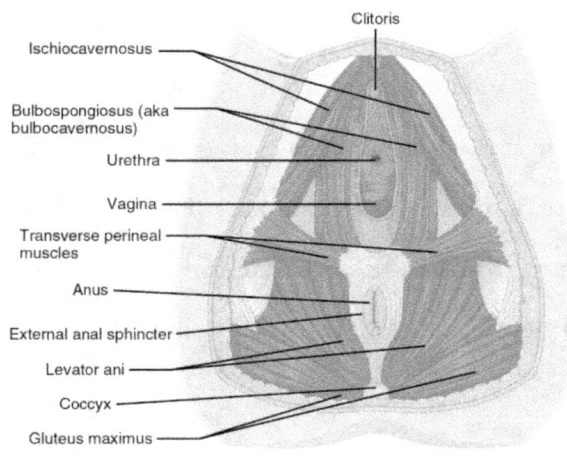

Diagram of the major pelvic floor muscles. This is the most superficial layer. Source: Wikimedia Commons.

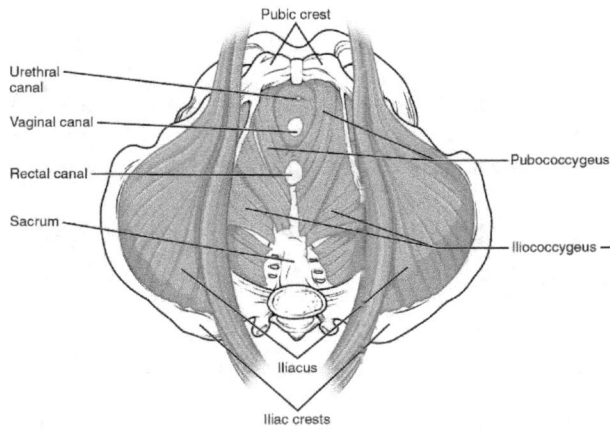

Diagram of the major pelvic floor muscles. This is the deepest layer. Superior view (from above). Source: Wikimedia Commons.

It can be difficult to understand this area from a book, so do your best to look at images, feel your own body, and orient yourself slowly. In the end, what matters most is how you feel, not knowing the name of a muscle you encounter. However, I've listed my favorite pelvic anatomy books in Resources if you want to dive deeper and view illustrations from multiple angles.

Sacred Pleasure Areas

Both internally and externally, the genitals contain many areas of pleasure. Some are well-known, such as the clitoris and G-spot, and others, like the a-spot, are less talked about. But ultimately, pleasure can be found anywhere. In *Vagina* by Naomi Wolf, the author shares that every woman has a unique nerve arrangement throughout the pelvis and genitals, which affects where she feels sensation [10].

It's important not to become too attached to the idea of fixed pleasure maps. The body is incredibly adaptable and can easily awaken sensation in previously "numb" areas with gentleness and presence. We are all capable of building sensitivity and feeling pleasure in different areas of the body.

In recent decades, researchers have learned that the clitoris is not just a small external organ but has internal "legs" called crura that extend beneath the labia and around the vaginal canal. In total, the clitoris is nearly five inches long.

The external part we see is just the tip of the iceberg. Incredibly, this wasn't even documented until 1998, when urologist Helen O'Connell mapped it in detail for the first time [11].

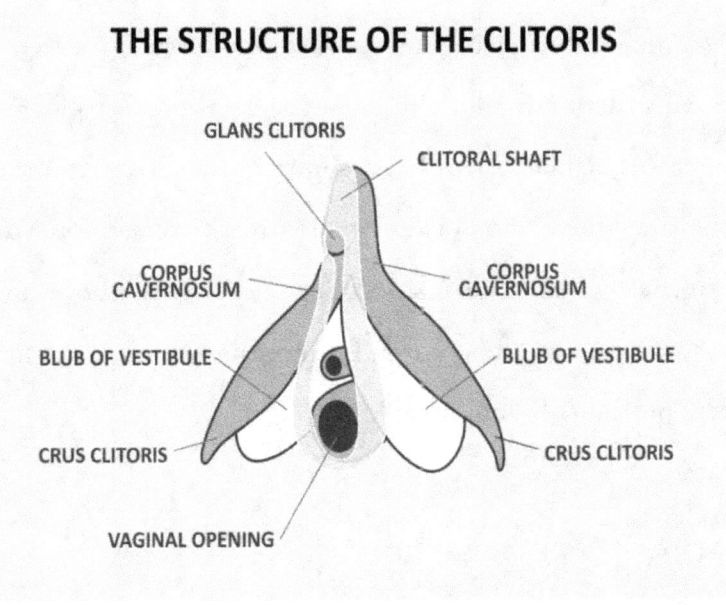

Image of the internal clitoris. Source: Dennissenko Oleg.

Many areas you might think of as separate from the clitoris are not. Because of its length and size, orgasms that result from stimulation to the inside of the vagina are usually contacting part of the clitoris's internal structure. For instance, the G-spot isn't a single point, but an area that includes clitoral tissue among other structures. Deeper erogenous zones near the cervix have been recognized (such as the a-spot), and likely all of these include at least some clitoral tissue or contact.

Anatomical knowledge can be empowering. It gives a sense of orientation and helps begin to awaken sensation. But everyone's internal structure is a little different, so let yourself explore with openness. The body's tissues are continuous and interconnected, so in reality, there's no isolation in movement or sensation. And it doesn't really matter what something is called, it's about how it feels to you. Always follow your instincts above a map, and it may lead to profound healing and pleasure.

Breasts

Breasts are an essential part of female health and are considered an accessory organ of the reproductive system.

Breast massage is a great practice for vitality and hormonal balance. The breasts are rich in lymph nodes, especially around the armpits and chest. Breast tissue extends farther than many people realize, reaching up toward the collarbone, into the armpits, and across the chest. Light massage promotes lymph movement, supporting both breast health and immune function. There are many reasons to incorporate breast massage into your self-care routine, from energetic nourishment to physical detoxification.

Breast massage stimulates the circulation of blood and lymph. Lymph fluid contains white blood cells, and lymph nodes act as filters, but its flow depends on external movement, such as walking, bouncing, or massage.

The breast tissue can store environmental pollutants, especially when constricted by tight bras or when exposed to non-natural deodorants and antiperspirants. Regular massage supports detoxification through increased blood flow and lymphatic movement.

In one study published in the Journal of Sexual Medicine, researchers used fMRI to observe brain activity as women touched different parts of their bodies. Stimulation of the nipples activated the same brain regions as the vagina, clitoris, and cervix, offering more evidence of the heart–pelvis connection [12].

These are just a few of the physical benefits of breast massage. But there is another layer: this heart-centered practice is deeply healing to the feminine spirit.

Most women, especially before becoming mothers, have only experienced touch here either in a clinical way or in a sexual context. What would it be like to explore this area with the intention of self-love and care?

You'll find a simple breast massage practice in Chapter 6. For now, let this be a reminder that your breasts are an essential part of your feminine wholeness and contribute to your vitality just as much as your womb or pelvic bowl.

Bring both hands to your heart, connecting to the radiance that lives here. Your heart is a channel for universal love. Let yourself soften and feel this space glow with the powerful energy that lives within you

.

Integration

Mapping your body is an act of reclamation. Learning about your physical structure supports your embodiment and builds the foundation for deeper presence and healing. As you cultivate this mind-body awareness through the meditations in this book, you begin to create real, felt shifts.

1. After learning more about your body and its structures, what area do you feel intuitively drawn to working with?
2. When you place your awareness in your pelvic bowl, what sensations or emotions come up? What images?
3. How does it feel to imagine a channel of energy between your heart and your womb? What longings live there?

3

Energetic Anatomy

Reconnecting to the Cosmic Womb

The Tao is like a well:

Used but never used up

It is like the eternal void:

Filled with infinite possibilities.

It exists everywhere and anywhere,

Hidden but always present.

I do not know who gave birth to it

It existed before Heaven and Earth

TAO TE CHING

T he womb pulses with aliveness. As a sensitive bodyworker, I began to notice that different areas of the body held distinct energy signatures. The womb felt entirely unique, unlike muscles or fascia, more alive than any other organ. There is a frequency here that speaks.

This chapter continues your journey inward, from physical form to subtle energy. In the previous chapter, you learned about the terrain of the pelvic bowl, with some energetic elements woven throughout. Now, you deepen into the unseen. The energetic landscape of the pelvis and womb are just as vital for your healing. It is in this space that you access your own knowing and power.

The pelvic bowl is a container for inspiration and transformation. It holds and links to your energetic essence, the soul of you. Though this can feel intangible, who you are is a makeup of your inherent spirit and your personality of this life: the stories that make up who you are, the lineage that runs through you.

There's a life force that is felt here. When you're falling in love, being moved by beauty, or becoming immersed in creation, you're touching the depth of that vital energy. When you engage in things that bring you joy, it's life-giving and soul-nourishing.

This life force within your pelvic bowl is powerful. It's the source of your vitality and creativity. It invigorates and inspires all you do and creates life itself. You can access this energy here, but it comes from something vaster, flowing to us from the cosmos.

My understanding of feminine energetics is rooted in our bodies and how we relate to the world around us. It also comes from my lived experience as a bodyworker and energy worker.

Many cultures have recognized that we are a woven network of body and spirit. Ancient systems like Chinese medicine and Ayurveda mapped the pathways through which energy moves in the body—called meridians in China and *nadis* in India. This vital energy is known as Qi, prana, or simply spirit, and flows throughout the body, especially concentrated in the pelvis for women [1].

In this chapter, you'll learn about the energy centers of the pelvis, foundational qualities of the feminine, and expand into a cosmic weaving of physical and spiritual. These energetic centers shape how you embody your deepest self.

The Energetic Landscape of the Pelvis

Chakras are an ancient yogic concept of energy centers in the body, now woven into many healing traditions around the world. The word *chakra* comes from a Sanskrit term meaning "spinning wheel of light". While this word originates from the Hindu tradition, awareness of energy centers exists worldwide, including within the Kabbalah, some Native American, Chinese, and Maya cultures. Though the number and descriptions vary, many traditions describe similar locations and energetic themes [2].

In the Hindu tradition, the seven chakras are concentrated energy centers along the *nadis*, subtle pathways similar to the meridians in Chinese medicine. The *nadi* system is incredibly intricate, said to include over 72,000 channels through which prana flows—not only through the physical body but also the energetic and spiritual realms. Unlike acupressure points, chakras don't have precise anatomical locations. In ancient Tantric texts, these centers are seen as a path to enlightenment, where cosmic energy is brought down from the crown to the root, and Earth energy is drawn upward. Life force spirals through the body along this channel, and this free flow is said to create more health and vibrancy.

Each chakra is important and shares a connection with each other, but here, I focus on the two lower centers held within the pelvic bowl: the root and sacral chakras. You can read more about other centers in the book *Energetic Anatomy* by Cyndi Dale.

Root Energy Center

The root energy center is located at the cervix for women and extends throughout the pelvic floor muscles. The root is associated with safety and your most basic human needs. When you feel connected and alive here, you can ground yourself into the Earth and draw from deep stores of strength.

This is the center that asks: Are your physical needs met? Do you feel a sense of safety in the world? What's the state of your energy levels and personal power? Do you trust life to provide? Do you feel alone, or an integral part of something larger?

When there's an imbalance here, there's a sense of feeling ungrounded, anxious, fearful, or caught in cycles of survival-based stress.

These deeper themes are contacted when massaging or meditating on these areas. Memories and emotions may arise. Each time you bring awareness to this area, each time you send love into your body or release a layer of pain or fear, you're doing the work of healing.

It's not always easy to face the past, but doing so builds the foundation for greater joy, love, and interconnectedness. Healing and working with the root opens the path to deeper trust in yourself, your body, and in life itself.

Womb Energy Center

As you rise from the root, you come to the womb energy center, also known as the sacral chakra. This center is located at the level of the uterus, ovaries, and sacrum, and it's associated with creativity, sexuality, and our emotional world. In Sanskrit, its name means "dwelling place of the self."

A central theme of this area is surrender—the ability to flow with life, and to be flexible. This often only comes after root healing and developing a foundation of safety and trust.

This center also holds the energy of relationships. This includes romantic and social connections, and your relationship with the Creator (if resonant to you). Your faith, healing journey, generosity, and capacity for gratitude are all explored here.

This center is the spark of your life force. Feeling a lack of creativity, or fatigue, numbness, depression, or experiencing reproductive issues on any level can indicate a need to work here. Nearly all the practices in this book help you work towards healing within this chakra.

Opening a healthy connection to your womb energy center allows you to experience harmony in your life. It awakens the magnetic feminine energy within you, allowing you to fill your cup and feel resourced. This is the life force that powers inner joy.

When your basic survival needs are met, you become available for the natural flow of giving and receiving in relationships. This wellspring of energy supports the development of all the chakras above and their themes: personal power, love and compassion, clear communication, inner vision, and spiritual connection.

These brief introductions to the root and womb centers offer a deeper framework for understanding yourself as both a physical and subtle being and will support your experience with the practices in this book.

Knowing that themes like fear, safety, depression, or numbness may surface (especially during pelvic massage) can help you meet the experience with mindfulness and compassion. Awareness is always the first step in healing.

In the following meditation, the framework of the chakras are explored to connect deeper with your energetic body and find another layer of understanding.

Connecting with the Root and Womb Centers

Lying down in a comfortable and warm place, place both hands over your yoni.

Start to bring your full awareness into your root—visualizing your pelvic floor, yoni, tailbone.

Center your awareness within your cervix as the heart of your root, imagining it fill with a healthy, ruby-red glowing light.

Breathe into this area and allow yourself to receive any messages here. Do you feel supported, trusting? Fearful, worried?

Visualize a cord of connection from your root down into the Earth. Allow yourself to release your worries and gather in deep grounded strength. Work with this visualization until you feel at peace in your body.

Next, travel up to the level of the womb energy center.

Breathe into this area and be open to receive any messages here.

Do you feel a sense of curiosity, aliveness? Or is there dullness, numbness?

Bring your full awareness here and visualize the area filling with a sparkling orange light. With this light, you awaken your vital essence.

Draw in life force from the Earth through the cord connecting you.

Connect to the whole of your feminine centers within your pelvic bowl.

Keep imagining them glowing with sparkling life.

Give thanks to your body.

Throat–Yoni Connection

The throat and yoni mirror each other. The vocal cords resemble the vaginal opening and are linked through the vagus nerve, which connects the brainstem to the cervix and supports a sense of safety in the body. The jaw and pelvis are connected through fascial connections, and tension in one often reflects in the other.

Sacred sound softens the pelvic floor and awakens the womb. Try the sounds "Ooo" (as in womb) and "Mmm," feeling the healing vibrations travel down into your pelvic center.

Womb-Heart Channel

The uterus is connected to the heart through an energetic channel known in traditional Chinese medicine as the Uterus Vessel, or *Bao Mai*. This channel is a reminder that the womb and heart are intimately linked in physical, emotional, and energetic ways. Emotions, intuition, sexuality, and love all move through this current.

When energy flows freely through the womb-heart channel, both reproductive and emotional well-being are supported. And stagnation can manifest as disconnection, whether it's from sensuality, self-love, or the body's deeper wisdom.

Your breasts are a gateway to this connection. When you massage them with presence and loving awareness, you activate the heart center and begin to awaken the womb-heart pathway. The more often you bring attention here, the more you soften into self-love that heals you.

Orgasm is another powerful way to nourish this channel. There is a natural upward flow of energy during climax, an ascending energy that can be guided with intention. During self-pleasure, visualize this energy flowing to your heart and bathing it in a pink, radiant light.

In Chapter 6, you'll find two practices that support this connection: the breast massage ritual and the Womb–Heart Spiral meditation.

In Chapter 8, I speak about how the heart–womb channel can be impacted by cesarean birth, and how postpartum practices can help restore the flow.

Core Feminine Energetic Qualities

Now that you've connected with these foundational centers, let's explore some of the core feminine energies I've noticed from working with women. Any woman can access these inherent patterns. Whether a woman is in her fertile years or not, the template is there: a cyclical and rhythmic aspect to her body she can rely on, a quality of receptivity, and a natural creative and birthing energy.

Cyclical Nature

Being in a woman's body is a lunar, cyclical experience. A woman with healthy cycles bleeds and ovulates throughout her fertile years, often in rhythm with the moon. Energies wax and wane as the month unfolds, mirroring the tides of the Earth and the pull of the moon.

Women's lives are deeply woven with the body's rhythms. They are always reminded of their body's connection to the natural world through the cycles of bleeding, the ten moons of pregnancy, the waves of birth, and the transitions that shape their lives.

Aligning with the Earth's cycles means embracing both rest and activity. The menstrual cycle moves through phases, each reflecting a seasonal rhythm. Understanding these phases helps you live in harmony with your true nature. These will be explored in depth in the next chapter.

Receptivity

A woman's energy is like an inward spiral, naturally receiving and drawing inward. This innate magnetism allows her to attract people, experiences, and energy toward her.

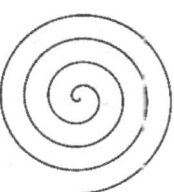

Receptivity does not mean passivity. It's about aligning with the flow of life. There are times for inspired action and setting the stage to fully receive. Aligning with this natural quality can bring abundance, fulfillment, and harmony to your life. Peace settles within your root when you realize you don't have to do everything yourself.

The uterus is a hollow organ whose powerful purpose is to receive and gestate life. To allow divine inspiration to come through into physical form. This receptive nature mirrors the energetic magnetism that flows through the female body.

The womb is an alchemical cauldron, a space for receiving and gestating. It can unconsciously hold stories and patterns or become a conscious vessel for what you choose to create. When you bring awareness here, you begin to reclaim some power.

In the Introduction, I mentioned how giving birth for the first time initiated me into a deeper openness than I had ever known. With this comes the possibility of abundance and miracles, and even developing psychic and shamanic abilities, but it must be balanced with an increase in boundaries and personal power.

In the Taoist tradition, as described by Mantak Chia, women's energy is seen as magnetic and receptive. These qualities give rise to creative expression and the fertility of motherhood. They have also made women natural healers, artists, and channels of divine energy.

Stories and myths are full of powerful, sultry women whose magnetism can't be resisted. Though these archetypes have often been twisted to demonize female sexuality, they hold a deep truth: this magnetism is a gift. One that can be harnessed to shape the life and world you wish to create.

Women, when they are in their full integrity and heart, can fill the world with vision and inspire others. This balanced female leadership is something the world needs greatly now.

This receptive nature is also what makes the womb such a potent storage place, particularly of wounds tied to shame, violation, sexuality, or negative feelings about being a woman. Many physical symptoms in the reproductive system are interwoven with these imprints.

Healing begins with mindful connection: placing hands on the womb, tuning in daily, engaging in healing practices, and bringing love to the space.

Just like you can receive harmful imprints, you may also receive love and goodness, and moments of beauty. These, too, live within the body.

In Chapter 6, the Cultivate Joy meditation is an example of one way to do this. Loving emotions and gratitude can be directed inward to nourish the body and spirit. This is how you rewrite core stories and remember that you are worthy of receiving.

Creativity

At the intersection of your physical and energetic body lies a powerful current: the creative potential of the womb. This energy lives in every woman, even in those who've had a hysterectomy.

This gestative and birthing pattern is mirrored in the menstrual cycle: the uterus builds for half the month (gestating), then releases (birthing). Women carry children and give birth. They envision projects and bring them to life. These innate qualities show up in many ways, and this energy can be harnessed for all forms of creation.

Practically speaking, ovulation is a potent time for creative projects. It's when energy, clarity, and radiance peak. Sexual energy can also be worked with as a tool: during orgasm, you can visualize your heart's desire and imagine sending it out through your body and into the world.

Creation requires both action and the discernment to know when it's time to surrender and receive.

To surrender means to soften and trust. To release the grip on how or when something will unfold. Whether or not we can do this reflects how much trust we carry in life, in others, and ourselves.

Surrender is receiving, and again, it's not totally passive; it can be an active harmonizing with life. It's essential for orgasm, birth, creation, and receiving support. And it can be cultivated. Here are a few ways to do this in your life:

Return to Nature

Spending time in wild places is one of the most direct ways to build trust in life. Go into a natural space whose beauty feeds your spirit. As you walk or sit on the earth, feel interconnected with the life around you.

Uncover the Stories

You can't force yourself to relax or receive without first understanding what stands in the way. Ask yourself:

- Growing up, did I feel safe, supported, or on my own?
- Do I believe the world is on my side, or that I have to work for everything?
- How have my life experiences affected my ability to trust?

Use Mantras to Repattern

After reflecting on your personal story, bring a hand to your heart or womb. Visualize your hand radiating warmth and a pink glow, infusing your body with these words. Use one of these, or create your own:

"I have complete trust in my body and the world around me."

"With each breath, I surrender and receive more and more."

Creation is not just action; it's also opening to receive the codes. Inspiration comes from this. When you come into the energetics of creation, you shift how you move through the world. You can start to feel supported by life. And in that receiving, life begins to mirror your trust, offering guidance and revealing the next steps.

Release

The womb is also an additional space where women can find release and renewal. This is both physical and energetic in nature. You will learn more about the physical aspect of release with each menstrual cycle in the next chapter.

You can understand creation as a cycle. There is a release and dissolution, then a rebirth. Again and again. Women experience this in their bodies, and it can be a powerful force to align with.

Each month when a woman menstruates, or when she releases a pregnancy or births a baby, she lets go of part of who she was. This happens in small ways each month but is particularly pronounced after women give birth (or experience miscarriage or abortion, which are also births). Each time the uterine lining is shed, she too can find emotional release and tap into a natural metamorphic process.

One way to align with this energy is through the luteal and menstrual phase of each month where one feels closer to their truth than ever. Let those emotions rise up and feel what needs to be felt. It is only through allowing ourselves to feel fully that we can let them go.

Creation isn't just about new life. It's one aspect of the cycle of life that things die, release, and are then re-born.

The Cosmic and Ancestral Womb

The womb is a portal. It connects you not only to creation, but also to the realm of the unseen: your female lineage. The womb carries both personal and ancestral memories. When you work with this area of your body, you contact something beyond you.

Your mother line spans the generations. It carries the codes of the physical body and can be a great source of support or a reminder of pain. Much of the time, it's both.

Many women carry trauma that began long before them. Some of it is personal, passed down through parenting patterns. Some are cultural, as the inheritance of patriarchy creates a deep feminine wounding. This brings shame and trauma into the body, and so there is a natural disconnection from the heart and womb. It shows up in how you were taught (or not taught) to relate to bleeding, birth, sexuality, and motherhood.

How many women have only heard positive sentiments about these rites of passage? How many have their womanhood celebrated, honored, and seen?

When you begin the journey of embodiment, you will eventually encounter the past. You may feel it stir inside of you as the voices of your grandmothers, the silent burdens they carried, and the wisdom they passed on.

Whether you know the stories of your ancestors or not, it lives within you. Your mother's story, her mother's story, and on. This work is not only to understand who you are, but to lighten the path for your children.

Across cultures, ancestral reverence was once woven into daily life: prayers, offerings, altars, and guidance-seeking. They knew that when they died, they would join their ancestors. They were never alone. Today, many of us feel a sense of drifted identity, as if there isn't a clear anchor to who we are. While there are possibilities within this openness, feeling connected to something more collective is also an important part of our humanity (and even nervous system well-being).

In every place I've lived, I've created an ancestor altar. Mine is devoted to the women in my line: my daughters, my mother, grandmother, and great-grandmother. I include photos, sacred art, candles, crystals, and a medicine bag that holds the dried umbilical cords of my daughters. Gifts from dear friends. I sit here and ask for guidance and protection. I offer my energy and love. I feel held by the women who came before me as I look at their photos.

I invite you to create your own ancestor or mother-line altar and fill it with things that are resonant with your spirituality and lineage.

And then in the upcoming meditation, you will journey even deeper into reconnection and the wisdom of the women before you.

Above all, in my work with women, I've seen miracle-level healing. Women who healed the kind of pain that they were told they needed a hysterectomy for. Spontaneous pregnancies after years of trying. Profound messages when contacting the womb. Angelic protection. Soul healing. This is the mystery that lives in the womb.

Mother Line Ancestral Journey

This is a deeper meditation, also called a journey, that will take you into the stories and wisdom of your mother line. Allow yourself not to have any expectations of what you'll find here, or what comes to you. Messages can be in the form of images, intuitions, or words. Receive it all and then reflect upon it later as you journal.

Playing a simple drumming track in the background helps access otherworldly states of mind. I love Sandra Ingerman's albums for this.

Begin by lying down in a comfortable place. Spend a few minutes deepening your breath, connecting to stillness within.

Start to feel the music and beat resonate through all the cells of your body, taking the space of any thoughts. Breathe.

Now imagine the beat transporting you to your favorite place in nature. You know this place intimately. Feel the air surrounding you, the Earth beneath you, scents and sights.

Start to become deeply centered within this sanctuary.

Feel yourself lying on the ground, deeply held by Mother Earth. She is your original ancestor and your home. Your body is made up of her body. Breathe, and feel the pulsing of the Earth surrounding you.

Start to travel back in time. Connect to the feeling of being in your mother's womb.

Breathe in the truth of whatever the story is between you. Let Mother Earth hold you.

Your mother now stands beside you in this nature sanctuary you are in. She looks at you with deep love. Does she have a message for you?

Now your grandmother appears next to your mother. She looks at both of you with deep love. Does she have a message for you?

Call in her mother next, and then her mother, and connect to each one. Hear each message. Imagine they are forming a circle around you, all looking at you with love. Spend some time living this.

Then, when you have generations of your mother-line surrounding you and have heard the messages from each of them, bring in your daughters, or the next generation of daughters. They are in the center of the circle, holding hands with you.

Feel the pure love within you. Look at the faces of your mother line. Know that they are always with you.

What strength, what wisdom, are you inheriting from them?

An elder comes forward to give you a blessing, a gift to remind you of this love, protection, and strength. Hold it in your hand and feel its radiance. Embrace her.

Then watch as each mother hugs her child, then her child, continuing down the line. Something is being healed here.

As you embrace your daughters, or the next generation, imbue them with that promise and hope, powerful feminine essence, and all its gifts. Hand them the blessing you were given. It is theirs to hold.

Then lay back down on the ground, embraced by Mother Earth. These daughters lie beside you, and all your mothers and grandmothers hold the space around you. Breathe in this circle of community.

Hold this vision and love for as long as you like.

When you feel ready, start to come back into your body, feeling the blessing and healing that has taken place. Take as much time as you like, with your hands on your womb and ovaries, your physical body connecting you to your maternal line.

As you return from this journey, may you know you are always held and supported by this long line of strong women.

You are never alone.

Integration

As you begin to attune to your energetic landscape, feel how your body responds. You may notice subtle shifts like sensations, memories, or the awakening of inner knowing. This space is alive, holding messages uniquely meant for you. Let it be a source of guidance you return to, again and again.

1. Do these feminine energetic concepts resonate with you? Are there aspects that feel less true for you, or qualities you would add?
2. In the Mother Line Ancestral Journey, what was the blessing item your elder gifted you? How did it feel to receive it?

4

Cyclical Wisdom

Living in Deeper Alignment and Rhythm

*The psyches and souls of women also have their own
cycles and seasons of doing and solitude, running and
staying, being involved and being removed, questing
and resting, creating and incubating, being of the world
and returning to the soul-place.*

CLARISSA PINKOLA ESTÉS

The first time I placed my hands on my womb during a guided group meditation, something profound happened. I had always sensed there was much to be listened to and worked through here. At one point, we were guided to listen to what our womb wanted. The answer was so clear: I wanted to have children.

Before that moment, the answer wasn't so clear. I lived a nomadic, free-spirited life, focused on my own healing. But after that meditation, everything shifted. My future children became the motivation. For my healing, for grounding, for creating a life that could offer them love and intention.

This pelvic voice is like the gut instinct, but deeper and more uniquely feminine. It's a felt sense in the body that knows when something is aligned, and when it's not. The more you learn to listen, the clearer it becomes. This voice is a woman's deepest source of intuition and can be her north star.

This chapter will end with a meditation that helps awaken your pelvic voice. But first, we begin with connecting to the rhythms of the womb.

Life becomes more easeful when working with the natural energy patterns of the body. When you're not aligned with the body's rhythms, life can feel harder than it needs to.

This isn't just about tracking fertility, though for many, that's where the journey begins (and it's important knowledge). This chapter is about aligning with nature itself.

Many women carry maiden wounds. Few were met with celebration at their first bleed. Instead, they may hold stories of embarrassment, secrecy, or shame. Many girls start on hormonal birth control early, beginning a decade-long (or more) disconnection from the body's cyclical nature and deeper messages.

If all you know is suppression of your natural rhythms, you will have little trust in your body. This loss of self-trust is one of the deepest maiden wounds. Re-connection begins with reverence. Then, body literacy and sovereignty restore embodied power. Reclaiming excitement to know yourself is healing to your inner maiden.

Your cycle is one of the most tangible ways to come home to yourself. This chapter explores the four phases of the female (fertile) cycle: what's happening physically, how your energy shifts, the season and archetype that align with each, supportive herbs, and reflection prompts.

As you move through these phases, notice where you may hold judgment or preference. Learn to appreciate the wisdom of all seasons of life.

As women close their fertile years, the cycle shifts into a new and profound season. I haven't yet walked this path, so I can only speak to it as seen from the outside in my work. There are specific energetics and emotions to work through here. I recommend reading the *Wisdom of Menopause* by Christiane Northrup to be guided in this rite of passage.

Trust the wisdom of your body to lead you, not just through your cycle, but also through the pivotal moments of womanhood. Think of a memory of instinctual knowing. Can you feel gratitude for all your body does for you?

Menstruation

Affirmation: I thank my body for all it does for me

A woman's cycle begins with menstruation, the Inner Winter. The uterine lining (endometrium) releases, bringing on bleeding and initiating a new cycle. This phase typically lasts around five days. Progesterone, the hormone that builds the uterine lining and supports pregnancy, drops as the lining is released. The cervix sits low, firm, and slightly open to allow this flow.

This is when the body needs to slow down, retreat inward, and listen. Feeling tired is the body's wisdom speaking. Outside of daily obligations, let yourself lean into what feels nourishing, restful, and contemplative.

In modern life, women are often expected to move through bleeding as if nothing has changed. But their desires, mood, and energy change throughout the month. At this time, there's a natural desire to rest.

When you ignore the call to stillness, the body often speaks louder. Painful cramps or deep exhaustion may be its way of demanding rest. The first step toward more easeful periods is learning to slow down. This is a time for nourishing activities: art, gentle movement, ritual baths, or quiet time in nature.

Say no to what doesn't feel right. Look for small ways to restructure your life and carve out space for yourself during this sacred time.

The archetype of Persephone lives within this phase. As the daughter of the Earth Mother Demeter, she was taken to the underworld by Hades. She lives half the year below the Earth, and half above, returning each spring to awaken life.

While this myth is often viewed as a story of patriarchal domination, it also reflects the soul's (and seasonal) cyclical journey of descent, darkness, and transformation. Like menstruation, it mirrors the feminine initiation: the underworld as a space for evolution and wisdom-gathering. It's a woman's vision quest.

Menstruation Herbal Support

- Cramp Bark: A powerful uterine relaxant that helps ease tension and soothe cramps. *Take as a tincture:* Take 1–2 dropperfuls at the first sign of cramping.
- Ginger: Warming, anti-inflammatory, and supports digestion. *Drink as a golden milk latte*: Simmer a few slices of fresh ginger in 1–2 cups of water for 10–15 minutes. Strain, then stir in ¼ teaspoon of turmeric, a pinch of black pepper and cinnamon, a splash of milk, and honey to taste.
- Yarrow: This herb supports healthy menstrual flow and strengthens energetic boundaries. *Use in a bath:* Combine with rose and lavender for a soothing bath. Add a tablespoon of each to a large cotton bag, steep in a quart of

boiling water for 15-20 minutes, then add the infusion to a bath.

Inner Winter Reflections

1. What am I needing to release this month?
2. What do I need to say no to in order to protect my rest?

Follicular

Affirmation: I approach life with trust and courage

Just after bleeding ends, you enter the follicular phase, the Inner Spring. The body begins preparing for the possibility of new life by rebuilding the uterine lining. Follicle-stimulating hormone

(FSH) rises, stimulating ovarian follicles to mature (which contain eggs). As ovulation nears, cervical fluid shifts to a clearer, stretchier consistency, and the cervix opens and softens. Estrogen and testosterone increase, and with them, energy and clarity re-emerge.

This time mirrors the feeling of stepping out of the winter cave and re-entering life. It's the energy of the waxing moon, growing toward fullness. There's a distinct sense of emotional openness, courage, and the hope that comes with new beginnings. This is a time of potential.

By following the rhythms of your body, you remember that you are a mirror of the natural world. Seasons shift and change, and there is purpose in both the underworld journey and the emergence.

The archetype of Flora lives in this phase. She is the Roman goddess of flowers, gardens, and spring. Flora reminds you to celebrate what is coming to life within you.

Follicular Herbal Support

- Nettle Leaf: Rich in minerals, nettle deeply nourishes the body after menstruation. It supports adrenal health and replenishment. *Drink as a tea:* Steep 1 tablespoon of dried nettle in hot water for at least 15 minutes. Drink in the morning to give gentle energy.

- Red Clover: An herb that supports hormonal balance and liver detoxification. Red clover is also associated with new beginnings. *Use in a tea blend or tincture form:* Combine with nettle or raspberry leaf for a supportive follicular-phase tonic: see below.

- Red Raspberry Leaf: A uterine tonic that strengthens and tones the womb. Traditionally used to support menstrual health and fertility. *Drink as tea:* Excellent as part of a daily springtime infusion: blend 1 teaspoon each of: nettle, red clover, and red raspberry leaf. Steep in 2 cups of boiling water for 15-20 minutes. Strain and drink 1-2 cups per day during the follicular phase.

Inner Spring Reflections

1. How can I use this blossoming energy to manifest my dreams?
2. What seeds am I planting in this cycle?

Ovulation

Affirmation: I am radiance

After spring comes your Inner Summer, the ovulatory phase. This is when an egg is released from the ovary in response to a rise in luteinizing hormone (LH) and follicle-stimulating hormone (FSH). Ovulation occurs around halfway in the monthly cycle, varying with each woman.

The fertile window (the few days leading up to and including ovulation) is the time when fertilization can occur. For those wishing to conceive or avoid pregnancy, understanding this window and the signs of ovulation is essential. Cervical fluid becomes clear and stretchy to support sperm transport, and the cervix rises, softens, and opens. See Resources for a recommended book on the Fertility Awareness Method.

Like summer, the energy of ovulation is hot, full, and expansive. This is the peak of your fertility and vitality. It's often the most extroverted and magnetic time of the month, and is ideal for connection, creativity, movement, and heart-centered expression. This is the phase of the full moon.

The archetype of Pele, the Hawaiian goddess of fire and volcanic creation, lives in this phase. She embodies passion, power, and metamorphosis. Pele teaches how to awaken the power of your inner voice.

Ovulation Herbal Support

- Rose: A softener of both the womb and the heart. Rose supports self-love and also teaches the importance of self-protection in balance with openness. *Use as a flower water spray.*
- Hibiscus: Hibiscus supports circulation and vibrant energy and is rich in antioxidants. *Drink as a tea blend:* Combine 1 teaspoon dried hibiscus, ½ teaspoon dried lemon balm, and ½ teaspoon spearmint. Steep in 2 cups of boiling water for 10-15 minutes. Strain and enjoy as warm or chilled tea.
- Shatavari: A traditional Ayurvedic herb known as a tonic for the feminine system. Supports libido and hormonal balance. *Use as powder:* Blends well in coffee or cacao lattes. Take ¼-½ teaspoon daily during ovulation if working on fertility or sensual awakening.

Inner Summer Reflections

1. What radiance am I wanting to share or express?
2. What are the current desires emanating from my womb?

Luteal

Affirmation: I trust in the ebb and flow of life

The luteal phase, your Inner Autumn, is the last phase of the cycle; a time of quiet before menstruation returns. It carries the energy of the waning moon, a turning inward toward darkness.

If conception occurs, progesterone rises to nourish and thicken the uterine lining. Basal body temperature remains elevated in early pregnancy. If fertilization doesn't occur, estrogen and progesterone drop, initiating the release of the endometrium and the start of a new cycle. The cervix becomes firm and closed, and cervical fluid becomes thicker and stickier in texture.

This is a time to sow seeds of self-care, so that when bleeding begins, you can fully rest without pain or depletion. It's also an ideal time for womb care rituals like pelvic steaming, which help prepare the body for release.

The luteal phase is an oracular time. In my work with women, the sessions where I had the strongest channel to insights were right before I was going to get my period. I was in a state of grounded power more than other times of the month. Many women find their truth rising to the surface during this time. You can trust what's coming through.

In this phase, you can connect with the archetype of Kuan Yin, the beloved goddess of compassion. Known as "she who hears the cries of the world," she offers protection through childbirth, motherhood, grief, and healing. Kuan Yin invites you to meet yourself with grace and a good amount of compassion as deep emotions surface.

Luteal Herbal Support

- Oatstraw: Mineral-rich and deeply calming, oatstraw supports and rebuilds. *Use as an infusion:* Steep 1 tablespoon in hot water for 30 minutes to several hours. Drink throughout the day.
- Milky Oats: Helps soothe strong emotions, nervous tension, and irritability. *Use as a fresh plant tincture:* 1–2 dropperfuls daily (best used long-term, at least a month).
- Motherwort: A deeply grounding herb for emotional overwhelm or rage. It supports the heart, womb, and nervous system. *Use as a tincture:* Take a dropperful as needed in times of emotional intensity.

Inner Autumn Reflections

1. What is no longer in alignment?
2. Is there a season or phase I tend to resist? Why?

Cyclical Pain

Many women live with cyclical pain that ranges from a few hours of cramping to debilitating symptoms they dread each month. For some, it's so bad that they consider hysterectomy. If you're navigating intense menstrual pain, including endometriosis, I encourage you to explore the books in the Resources section at the back of this book.

In choosing to align with the wisdom of the body, you can understand strong cramping as a signal: the uterus is working hard to clear out congestion. This can be a call to work more deeply with the health of your pelvic organs, reducing inflammation, and supporting its circulation.

Here are some of what I've seen to be the most helpful in supporting painful cycles:

- Abdominal Massage: This softens tissue, supports digestive health, and encourages more complete uterine cleansing. Over time, many women find that consistent massage helps alleviate painful cycles.
- Castor Oil Packs: Castor oil reduces inflammation and scar tissue while stimulating blood and lymph flow.

These actions support hormonal balance and reduce the stagnation that often contributes to painful periods. See Chapter 6 for full guidance on this practice.

- Herbal Pelvic Steaming: A deeply relaxing ritual that stimulates circulation, eases pelvic congestion, and can help reimprint the womb space, from pain into warmth and pleasure. See Chapter 6 for full guidance on this practice.
- Nutritional Shifts: Painful periods have been linked to a zinc and magnesium deficiency. Make sure to take optimal, bioavailable forms: a whole-foods oyster or chicken liver supplement, along with magnesium glycinate. Herbs that have been shown to be helpful with painful periods are ginger, cramp bark, and motherwort.

When you're in pain, it's easy to feel overwhelmed or hopeless. But pain is also communication and is always a call for deeper attention and tending. Committing to these practices can support your body in clearing stagnation and restoring balance. Healing is possible.

Awaken Your Pelvic Voice Meditation

This meditation is inspired by the one that awakened me years ago. May it offer you a return to the wisdom that already lives within you.

It creates space for the stories, emotions, and imprints held in the pelvis to be brought into conscious awareness. This practice deepens your connection to your pelvic voice, where your wisest self resides.

Allow yourself time to prepare, and space afterward to journal and integrate. For many, this is the first moment of hearing their womb speak, and it can be profoundly emotional.

Cultivating this connection strengthens intuition and sensitivity for the deeper practices in the book.

This is a beautiful practice to revisit seasonally. And in daily life, you can return to it in small ways, like simply placing a hand on your womb when you need guidance, remembering that there's a wise voice within you that you can always access.

Begin by setting the space with intention and the energy of ritual. Find somewhere quiet. Light candles or incense. Let yourself feel open, receptive, and curious.

When you're ready, lie down in a comfortable place. Take time to breathe and relax your body. Then you can begin.

Place both hands on your womb. Feel warmth beneath your hands, the space filling with radiant, crystalline light.

With each exhale, allow this light to expand through your uterus, uterine tubes, ovaries... and down to your cervix and yoni.

Let the warm, glowing light travel and spiral down through your thighs, knees, and lower legs... all the way to the bottoms of your feet.

From the soles of your feet, a cord extends, connecting you to the deep core of the Earth.

You begin to spiral down, descending through each layer of the Earth.

Now you have reached the core of the Earth. You have arrived at a portal.

Mother Earth has been waiting for you. She welcomes you.

You rest on the rich soil—safe, grounded, held.

You are here to listen. To the voice of the body, the voice of the womb you were born with and blessed to carry.

With each breath, you begin to travel back in time.

You return to the womb of your mother. How does your mother feel about being full with the life of you?

Now see the scene of your birth. Witness how you were received into the world.

How were you nurtured or not in your early years? Breathe...

Now see yourself as a girl, the first time your sexual energy began to awaken.

Was it met with innocence or shame?

Now recall your first period. What was it like for her then? Listen.

Now you come to your first sexual experience.

Ask your womb if there's anything she wants to share with you about a lover, or an experience that still lives within her.

Now, bring your awareness to your current lover. How does that feel in your body?

Mother Earth is still with you. You are safe. You are deeply grounded.

Breathe.

Ask your womb: How does she feel about pregnancy? Birth? Motherhood?...

Are there any imprints or dis-ease within her? How can you support her healing and vitality? Just listen.

Now let your womb speak on anything. Be open to whatever comes.

When you're ready, thank your body for speaking. Your soul-voice has been heard.

You are lighter.

When you feel ready to return... Mother Earth helps you rise.

You remain connected to her through the cords in your feet, spiraling upward, layer by layer, back from her deep underground well.

Feel your womb beneath your hands, the heat. Smile.

Send that warmth to every cell in your body. Let your heart radiate with compassion. You are whole—and always have been.

This connection remains with you. The pathway has been awakened.

Integration

Living in alignment with your inner rhythms is radical in a culture that doesn't make space for the full spectrum of the female experience. We're taught to only value the outward, productive phases, while ignoring the wisdom in the inward and unseen. Feel the difference as you move into self-trust, honoring your cyclical nature as both compass and guide.

1. What phase of your cycle do you struggle with the most? What phase do you love being in the most?
2. What was the strongest wisdom that was transmitted to you in the closing meditation?

5

Clearing and Re-Patterning

Healing Trauma Held in The Pelvis

The doors to the wild self are few but precious. If you have a deep scar, that is a door, if you have an old, old story, that is a door. If you love the sky and water so much you almost cannot bear it, that is a door. If you yearn for a deep life, a full life, a sane life, that is a door.

CLARISSA PINKOLA ESTES

This chapter is all about the emotions that often come up when women enter the territory of their pelvic bowl. It offers an introduction to what may surface and how to process and integrate those emotions before beginning the embodiment practices. This guidance is meant to help you make sense of what emerges and support your transformation as you work with what lives in your body.

In my experience, it feels incomplete to share practices focused on the pelvic space (which is often a deeply charged area) without first addressing the emotions held here. Without that foundation, you might feel frustrated or overwhelmed by what comes up, without the opportunity to move through the stuckness and trauma into the vitality that lies on the other side.

What lives within you, what you are made of, is both personal and societal. Through considering what you've inherited, you can start to understand who you are more deeply. We live in a world that has long devalued women and the feminine. It has been many generations since there have been cultures that centered or appreciated traditional female domains: motherhood, caregiving, herbal medicine, community well-being, and living in rhythm with natural cycles. Alongside this, female experiences like bleeding and birthing have lost their sacredness. Now they are often viewed through a lens of shame or pathology, rather than being honored as powerful rites of passage.

Facing your shadows is an act of bravery. When you mine the depths of your sexuality, you arrive at the core of who you are, and you remember this truth: no matter what has happened to you, you are a divine being of love and purpose.

Through uncovering your shadows, healing shame, and reclaiming self-love, you empower yourself in a way that can never be taken from you. Your presence begins to shift your relationships and radiate what is possible. This is important, powerful work.

Healing unfolds in layers, arriving in its own timing. An emotion or memory may surface, and healing comes through feeling it fully instead of trying to fix or change anything. Every expression in your body has an origin.

In truth, there is no "getting rid of" emotion. You can suppress it, but eventually, it will circle around to be felt again. Every strong feeling carries a vital instinct beneath it. I invite you to sit with what comes to you, without judgment or rushing to find the story behind it. Healing begins when we honor ourselves enough to feel. And often, the intensity of the emotion shifts only when it's fully felt.

Somatic Awareness + Trauma in the Pelvis

The pelvic bowl is a potent storage site for unprocessed memories, emotions, and stress. If you've ever received a massage or been touched by a lover and suddenly recalled a forgotten memory, you've felt how deeply the body remembers.

Emerging research in somatic psychology from pioneers such as Dr. Peter Levine and Dr. Bessel van der Kolk affirms this connection between mind and body. Emotions, memories, and trauma leave imprints in our tissues [1].

Trauma is any experience that overwhelms someone's capacity to cope. In response, the body instinctively chooses a survival strategy: fight, flight, freeze, or fawn. For many women, freezing is most common, especially when their animal self knows they can't defend or escape. That freeze becomes an imprint; a pattern of tension that the body carries forward until resolved. It can show up as numbness in tissues, restricting energy flow and impacting physical health.

Another common response to a threat is fawning; becoming submissive and appeasing the perceived danger to avoid harm. While it may be a wise survival tactic, when it becomes your default, it can deeply erode a sense of self and boundaries.

Any perceived danger creates holding patterns in the body: muscular tension, collapsed posture, restricted movement or breath. Areas may feel numb or be in chronic pain cycles. The body becomes oriented to a state of hypervigilance instead of relaxation. Since many women's innate responses include freezing and fawning, this can show up as a deeply parasympathetic state— immobility, dissociation, or chronic fatigue. Rather than the outward activation of fight or flight, it's an internalized stillness, but not a healthy one. It's a paralyzed and numb state, one that requires action in order to heal.

Kimberly Ann Johnson explores this in-depth in her book *Call of the Wild*. She explains that women's trauma often shows up through freeze and fawn responses, which can make practices like stillness and meditation less helpful or even reinforcing of stuck patterns. Instead, she offers somatic tools focused on embodiment, gentle mobilization, and building nervous system capacity. Her work is an important resource if you want to go deeper into understanding and healing these patterns.

The emotional and physical weave together: unresolved experiences shape tissues, breath, the nervous system, and even one's sense of self.

This long-term survival state impacts women deeply, often without them realizing it. You may find that until you begin to soften into felt safety, you only recognize later how much tension you were carrying as a default.

Trauma imprints show up in numerous ways long after the event, but they all have one thing in common: they block access to full vitality. They often leave gaps in memory. The nervous system remains in high alert, creating tension and restricting flow. This can show up as pelvic floor tension, fascial restrictions, even scar tissue. The body's healing slows.

Traumatic experiences live within the body, but you don't need to know the stories to heal them. Simply being present with sensations and allowing yourself to move and feel freely helps release stored energy.

The practices in this book are meant to help you develop a deeper sense of bodily awareness and to recognize and work with emotions as they come up. These practices are meant to support nervous system restoration, and the books within the Resources section are highly recommended to go along with this information.

If something surfaces that feels like too much to hold on your own, seeking support is a brave next step. You may benefit from outside support if you notice:

- Frequent dissociation from your body
- Difficulty staying in the present moment
- Sudden waves of exhaustion or numbness
- A sense of disconnect or emotional wall between you and your body
- Feeling like you'd like more in-person emotional support and holding, and additional practices

Through my work with women, I saw patterns to the kinds of stories that come up when connecting to the pelvic bowl: memories of sexual experiences and pelvic procedures, births (including abortions and pregnancy losses), and internalized messages about womanhood. However, many more core memories and connections can be imprinted here as well.

As I've spoken before, just as you can hold pain, you can also hold joyful memories. You can re-imprint the pelvic bowl with love instead of shame, pleasure instead of fear.

One powerful way is through the imagery you hold during self-pleasure. Can the beauty of a sunrise bring you to climax and rewire your sensuality? Other moments include positive and loving sexual encounters, experiencing or witnessing a beautiful birth, and even shifting how you feel about your body. The possibilities are endless.

Emotional Imprints in the Body

Many emotions tend to come up when contacting the pelvic area—shame, rage, grief, love, and more. More than any other part of the body, this space holds a lot, for all the reasons explored up to this point. This section offers a grounded and gentle framework for meeting emotions as they surface.

The most important thing you can do when strong emotions come up is to stay present with them. Trust that they are here for a reason. Approach them with compassion and eventually gratitude, because emotions that stay buried will impact you physically and spiritually over time.

You can center yourself in the present moment by focusing on your breath and how it moves through your body. Let your awareness connect with the physical space around you. Appreciate emotions as self-protective. Acknowledge that this feeling belongs to the past, and you are safe now, at this moment. Fill your heart with self-compassion.

If you don't know where the emotion comes from, that's okay. Stay with the sensation rather than trying to uncover a memory. Let your breath circulate the energy throughout your body. If you need to cry or move, do it. Your body is wise, and these physical expressions help.

Ultimately, you know yourself best. Trust your sense of what you can move through on your own, and if you need more support, reach out to a therapist, ideally someone trained in somatic techniques (see Resources).

If you feel exhausted from running through the same emotions, and nothing seems to shift, try this: practice feeling yourself beyond the emotion. When something intense comes up, close your eyes and turn inward. Feel the sensation of that emotion, then imagine it like a leaf on a stream, or a wave in the ocean. It passes through, but it's not you. Emotions are fleeting. They are not the essence of who you are.

And take a break. Move your body. Get outside. Do something that makes you laugh or feel joy. Don't worry about any practice for today. Sometimes, healing isn't always about diving in but creating space instead.

The following pages explore common intense emotions that tend to come up, and how each can be understood and respected more deeply.

Anger and Rage

Anger and rage are healthy emotions and signs of vitality. When you feel angry, it often means a boundary was crossed, and you are mobilizing to protect what matters to you. Especially after a period of numbness, anger can signal that you're "coming back online."

These emotions want expression. Let them move through physical activity: dance, run, box, yell into a pillow. Use their fire to clarify what you will no longer accept in your life. What happened to you was not okay, but you can be free. You can be strong again.

Numbness

Numbness is an intelligent self-protective response. After experiencing something overwhelming, sometimes the only way to cope is to shut off emotions.

The first step is to thank your body for that protection. Then, slowly begin to explore what safety feels like again in your body. Healing numbness requires showing your nervous system that it's okay to feel again, which may take time. Ask yourself: *What would help me feel truly safe?*

For some, the answer might be financial security. For others, it may be changing living situations, setting boundaries, or leaving toxic relationships. The deeper work, too, is learning to trust yourself as your foundation.

And remember: discovering joy is part of this healing. Dream and create a life that makes you want to revel in it, not disconnect. Take even small steps in the direction of your heart's vision.

Grief and Sadness

Grief and sadness often come up when beginning this work. Women carry a lot: personal unmet needs, the silencing of mothers and grandmothers, the feminine diminished over generations.

Grief deserves time and space to feel and be listened to. Once there, it often brings you right into the center of life. One of the gifts of grief is that you become more fully human. At the same time, you come into contact with the soul, the most *real* part of you. There is an opportunity to be re-woven anew as a rigid attachment to identity releases.

Let yourself feel its depths and know that rebirth always comes after death. Your joy will become even more alive when you have experienced grief. It is up to us to discover our power and heart despite our external circumstances.

Longing

Longing is subtle but powerful. It often comes up when awakening the deeper layers of the heart and womb, when you begin to access inner pleasure or energy that you didn't know was possible.

Longing is a deep part of your soul remembering its desires. All the desires you have held within your subconscious can emerge when listening to your pelvic voice. These are not just your own longings, but those of the women who came before you.

It can feel like your desires are too much, but you can meet them. They are a sacred compass and point you toward your heart's truth.

Shame

Shame is common, often surfacing before you even begin. You may feel it when you touch yourself with presence, when you breathe deeply, and listen.

This shame isn't yours. It's the legacy from unhealthy, fractured cultures that feared the life-giving power of the female body.

When shame comes up, get curious. What's underneath it? Often, there's anger toward the person or system that made you feel unworthy. Or grief for how long you've been disconnected from yourself.

This is your opportunity to rewrite a different story. If you have a specific memory, re-envision it. Can you dream up how you wish it had gone instead? Say to yourself: *I love my body. I am powerful. I am whole.* Even better, choose a mantra that feels true and resonant for you.

Sexual and Birth Trauma

Of all the experiences that live in the pelvic space, sexual trauma is the most common story where outside support can be vital, especially if the violation happened in childhood.

Your child-self, in all her wisdom, dealt with overwhelming situations by learning to disconnect. Because of this, it can be hard to come home to your body; it doesn't feel like a safe place. Disconnection is what feels safe and familiar.

Start by appreciating the parts of you that kept you safe. Then, when you're ready, working with a somatic therapist can be incredibly helpful. I've also included a book recommendation in Resources for working through this deep trauma.

Another type of sexual trauma is birth trauma. When health providers dismiss you during birth, it leaves an imprint. When things are done to you without your consent, that's sexual assault. Industrial birth de-centers women in their pregnancies and facilitates the outcome of interventive and traumatic births. Birth has the potential to be the most powerful and ecstatic experience in a woman's life. It can be difficult to find someone to talk to who can help unpack this trauma without dogma. See Resources at the end of the book for a recommendation.

Herbal Support for Emotional Integration

- Lemon Balm (*Melissa officinalis*): This herb is like sunshine for the nervous system. It's uplifting and eases worries. It's a soothing balm for the heart. *Drink as a tea*: Combine 1 teaspoon each of lemon balm and linden, and steep in 1 cup of boiling water for 15 minutes.
- Tulsi, or Holy Basil (*Ocimum sanctum*): This beloved adaptogenic plant helps support emotional well-being and tends to your heart when you feel depleted or stressed. Tulsi calms and grounds. *Drink as a tea*: Combine 1 teaspoon Tulsi with ½ teaspoon lemon balm and a few rose petals, and steep in boiling water for 10 minutes.

- Milky Oats (*Avena sativa*): One of the best restoratives for the nervous system. It is deeply supportive during stress, exhaustion, and heals worn nerves. *Take as a fresh plant tincture*: Best as a long-term remedy: 1-2 dropperfuls per day for at least a month to support deep replenishment.
- Albizia (*Albizia julibrissin*): Known as "the tree of happiness" in Chinese medicine, this is a powerful remedy for grief and heartache, moving emotions that feel stuck. Albizia connects you to joy. *Best as a tincture*: take a dropperful as needed when grief surfaces, especially in the heart area.

Practices for Clearing + Repatterning

In addition to herbs, guided imagery and energy work can be powerful tools for clearing imprints held in the body. Once you've named what lives here, you can shift it. What follows are practices to begin this journey.

Because the pelvic bowl stores so many unconscious feelings and emotional remnants, a regular energy-clearing practice is deeply supportive.

After I gave birth, I naturally began doing energy work with women and slowly developed my own intuitive approach to pelvic clearing. I discovered that each woman carries her own healing symbols through inner imagery. Once she connects with them, her body begins a re-imprinting and healing process on its own. These are the spaces in which I learned so much about the energy of the womb and the common stories of women that weave us together.

After doing bodywork, I would place my hands over a woman's womb or ovaries and follow my intuition. I stayed open to receiving imagery or insights. I rarely spoke immediately. First, I guided her to enter her nature sanctuary and describe it to me. This helped anchor her in a safe and nourishing inner space that she could come back to again as needed.

Each session unfolded uniquely, but common themes emerged: stuck energy, symbolic imagery, and the presence of ancestors or guides. I would ask her to share any sensations or visions she received, and only after that would I offer what I had felt. If there was alignment, I invited her to breathe awareness into that area of her body.

Often, we would bring in a healing element from her sanctuary (like sunlight, a willow tree, the breeze by the sea) to re-imprint the space within her.

One woman I worked with came carrying the imprint of childhood sexual trauma that had happened after her mother's death. When I tuned into her right ovary, the image I received was of a dark, haunted house, with cobwebs everywhere. I asked her to stay present with the sensations and share what she was experiencing. When I sensed any distress, I guided her back to her nature sanctuary.

As she returned to that inner place, I immediately saw a vision: sunlight pouring through the fields, a joyful little girl barefoot in tall grass, picking flowers. I asked what she saw, and our images aligned. We used that light and innocence to fill the space in her body. Sunshine cleared the cobwebs, and childlike joy dissolved the heaviness of her pelvic space. Everything felt different, lighter.

As we moved through the imagery, tears welled up. I felt the presence of her mother and grandmothers, a deep knowing that they had always been there, protecting and holding her. She still carried their strength. I chose to share that imagery, and she nodded, tearfully saying, "I've always felt that."

This intimate story is one of many that illustrate how you can connect with your mystical, visionary self and follow the threads to your healing. Whatever comes to your mind will be unique to you and the perfect medicine in that moment to re-imprint your darkness into light. No one else can choose these soul-healing symbols for you. This is your mysterious template of health.

Pelvic Bowl Clearing Meditation

The pelvic bowl holds stories, feelings, and impressions. You can begin shifting these imprints through energy clearing and intuitive imagery. Trust that what you feel, imagine, or sense is valid, and your body is always seeking resolution.

Find a comfortable position, either seated or lying down. Place your hands over your womb. Begin to deepen your breath, letting your body settle into stillness.

Bring to mind a place in nature where you feel deeply at home. A place that feels safe and familiar to you.

What does it feel like to be there? What or who is around you? What do you hear? Smell?

You are safe here. This is your Nature Sanctuary. Return to this space anytime you feel overwhelmed or disconnected from your body.

Now, bring your awareness into your pelvic bowl.

Visualize this space filling with radiant white light—your pelvic bowl and the energetic field around it.

Let your whole consciousness settle here, as if your awareness is dropping from your head into your womb.

Notice any areas that feel dark, stuck, or heavy. Allow the light to pour into those places with softness.

As you stay with these denser areas, does any imagery come to you? Be open to receiving from your body's wisdom.

If imagery appears, allow it to bathe the areas of darkness. Feel your pelvic bowl illuminated, softened, and re-patterned.

You don't need to search for the stories. Just be present with sensation and bring in more radiant light and love.

If nothing comes to you, just bring the energy of happiness and safety from your Nature Sanctuary to come into this space in your body.

Remain in this visualization for several minutes until you begin to feel a sense of lightness or peace.

If at any point you feel overwhelmed, disassociated, or disconnected, return to your Nature Sanctuary. It's your anchor. If any imagery from that place feels meaningful, bring it into your pelvic space as medicine.

Only leave your sanctuary once you've gathered a felt sense of peace. Pause or stop this practice at any time.

When the energy in your body feels more spacious, when the darkness has softened, slowly bring your awareness back to the room.

Place one hand on your heart, and one on your womb.

You can return to this practice whenever you need grounding, energetic clearing, or reconnection with your inner voice.

Reclaiming Presence Meditation

This meditation helps you get in touch with how your body feels on a deeper level. At first, it may be difficult to maintain focus, but over time your perception of each part of your body will increase, and it will be easier to connect. This is a simple yet profound practice to work through numbness and expand awareness.

It's best done lying down so you can fully relax each part of your body and tune into your sensations. You may want to read it through once before or record it as an audio. It involves scanning from head to toe, with special attention on your pelvic space. Some people find guided audio helpful at first when it's difficult to focus.

As you begin to drop deeper into your body,

Your breathing slows, awareness moves internally, and the outside world becomes further and further away.

Breathe deeply, filling your lungs as your ribcage expands.

Exhale, and your ribcage contracts in all directions.

Thoughts are like ocean waves—crashing and receding.

You don't need to follow them. Just return to your breath.

Each exhale sinks you deeper into the ground beneath you.

Release all tension. All worry. Breathe.

You'll now scan through the body.

Inhale—create a little tension.

Exhale—soften and release.

Now continue up the body, slowly, one part at a time.

From your toes to your head...

Now bring one hand to your vulva, the other to your heart.

Let the warmth of your heart flow downward into your pelvic space. Breathe...

Now place both hands on your vulva.

How does this feel to you?

Let any emotion rise and fall like a wave. It comes and goes.

Feel the space below your hands begin to glow with soft pink light.

Let that light expand through your pelvic bowl—into the shadows, the numbness, the tension.

Let it soften and renew. Send light into any place that needs it.

Is there a message for you? Let it be heard.

The temple between your legs is your sanctuary.

It is where your soul voice lives.

No matter what has happened,

You are eternally yours. Erotically innocent.

Breathe in this truth as you exhale pleasure into your body.

You are connected.

Feel your heart fill with love and gratitude.

Integration

Letting go of old imprints that live in your body is profoundly healing. They block access to your full vitality and clarity. As you sit in presence with your body, you can honor what needs to be felt and release what isn't yours. And in that openness, something new can grow: grounded self-trust, emotional resilience, and a deeper connection to who you truly are.

1. When you connect with your pelvic bowl, what emotion feels most present out of the ones explored in this chapter?
2. What's your favorite form of self-care to feel grounded after working through intense emotions? Make a list to have on hand if you feel overwhelmed.
3. What came up for you in the Reclaiming Presence meditation? Did anywhere in your body feel tense or disconnected? Or most alive?

6

Practices for Pelvic Awakening

Embodied Rituals for Healing and Vibrancy

Feminine consciousness is a realm we can enter but not grasp. She pours her blessings on those who come to her in the spirit of surrender and service. If we undertake the quest in order to use her or control her, then her doors stay closed—and our psyche is separated from her source.

WOMB AWAKENING

As you begin to connect with your womb and pelvic area, it's important to first consider how you approach yourself within these practices.

Think of your pelvic bowl as a temple space. When you meet your body with slowness and respect, something begins to shift. The tissues soften and energy moves.

If you have the space for it, begin any self-care practice with ritual to help shift your consciousness. That might mean lighting a candle, setting an intention, or simply slowing your breath. What matters most is your presence. When your mind wanders, bring your attention back into your pelvic bowl, or wherever you're focusing at that moment.

As you explore the practices ahead, release pressure to follow my guidance exactly. Instead, focus on what you feel. Trust your body.

If anything feels too activating or overwhelming, pause. Give yourself grace and know that taking a break or stopping is always an option. Healing happens in trusting, not forcing. The practices in this chapter are offered in a progression:

1. *Awareness*: Begin with breathwork, meditation, and visualizations to anchor presence and notice sensation in your pelvic area.

2. *Opening*: Foundational practices that bring warmth, flow, and softening into the body.
3. *Alchemy*: The heart of this work—massage and bodywork for your feminine center, supporting transformation and deep healing.

Let's begin with entering the temple and grounding into the body. Before diving into the deeper bodywork practices ahead, you are invited to begin with something foundational: awareness.

Awareness

Without conscious breath and visualization, it's difficult to truly drop into the body. These practices are meant to help you build a relationship with your pelvic space. It's through this presence that your own voice can guide you through your healing.

Awareness is a skill that develops over time. At first your mind may wander. You might not feel much sensation. But each time you return your presence back to your body and bring in positive emotions and feelings, you do the work of re-patterning. Over time, you'll notice more subtle feelings and an awakening of life force.

With any pelvic care practice in this chapter, I suggest beginning with a simple meditation: place both hands on your womb (or one on your womb and one on your heart) and bring breath and love into your body. Connect to a sense of openness and deep presence, returning again and again. It's simple yet profound.

The following two meditations support this foundation. The Womb-Heart Spiral is a beautiful warm-up to any pelvic care practice. And the Cultivate Joy meditation is a longer, stand-alone practice, which includes elements of the spiral and can be used anytime you want to reconnect with the felt sense of love as a healing force.

Womb-Heart Spiral Meditation

Beginning the work to heal the pain and grief held in the feminine heart starts with connecting to compassion. Earlier chapters touched on the meridian pathway in Chinese medicine that connects the heart and the uterus, reflecting ancient knowledge of this important relationship.

Stress and emotions held in these areas of your body can impact you on many levels. Everything is connected, and wounds held within the heart affect your reproductive system and pelvic bowl.

What follows is one of my favorite meditations to encourage the mental and energetic connection between the heart and womb to promote healing and vitality to both centers. It's simple, but I have found it to be profound.

Start with one hand on your heart and the other on your womb.

On an inhale, breathe up the desire energy of your womb.

On an exhale, breathe down the fiery compassion of your heart.

Inhale up towards the heart, the wisdom of your womb.

Exhale down towards your womb, the sweetness of your heart.

Your heart is the arrow, the pool of Love,

Your womb is the deep feminine flame.

With each inhale, send the love and depth of your womb up to heal and bathe your heart.

On each exhale, send the love and fiery compassion of your heart to heal and bathe your womb.

Get into a rhythm, spiraling up and down, feeling their connection and qualities in tune with each breath.

Do this as long as you like.

Cultivate Joy Meditation

This meditation helps cultivate gratitude and joy as a deeply felt experience, which I believe are some of the most healing energies you can bring into your body. You can use this energy to inspire and invigorate you or send it to any part of your body that needs this medicine.

You'll notice this meditation weaves in the Womb-Heart Spiral near the end, connecting these feminine centers again.

For this meditation, start by lying down. Spend several minutes beforehand to get comfortable, tune into your breath, and start to quiet your mind. Then when you're ready, begin.

Bring both hands to your heart.

Feel the passion and fierce love that emanates beneath any hurt and fear. Feel your essential nature here.

With each breath, grow this love. See your heart beneath the stories of this one life.

Feel this love grow and rest your mouth into a smile.

Now focus your attention on your third eye, the point between your eyebrows.

This is our inner vision, where we can channel information and receive from the world.

Start to picture in your mind's eye someone you love. Visualize their face in all its detail, and feel your own smile grow.

Picture them smiling back at you, sending you the same love that you feel for them. Take in this image and love through your third eye point.

Keep imagining this for a few more breaths, deepening this inner picture.

Feel the smile on your face and the warmth in your heart from adoring this being who unconditionally adores you.

Now imagine that love as a bright light, bringing it down from your third eye center, down your throat and chest, all the way to your heart.

Feel the radiance of this light full of love in your heart. Sit with this for a few breaths.

Keep smiling.

When you're ready, send that light down to any parts of your abdomen or pelvic area that you feel need love and healing.

Connect to each place as you smile and feel the love being transmitted there.

When you're ready, still smiling and feeling the growing love within your body, bring that light further down to your uterus. Place both hands here now.

See the radiant light bathing your entire womb space. This unconditional love and compassion fill the space.

Breathe, smile, and feel that love grow.

You can put one hand on your heart now, with the other on your womb. Start to awaken the living connection between these two areas.

With each inhale, you breathe up the wisdom and beauty of your womb and your feminine nature to heal your heart.

With each exhale, you breathe down the fiery compassion of your heart to ignite and heal your womb space.

Feel the spiraling up and down with each breath, awakening a stronger connection each time. Keep smiling.

When you are ready, feel gratitude in your body on a visceral level.

Know that beneath any hurt, there is an unshakable core of love within you, always ready for you to come home.

Sacred Movement

Before moving into deeper touch or ritual, try some movement that opens up the hips. Do hip circles (standing or sitting), pelvic tilts, and butterfly pose (soles of the feet together, knees relaxed). These movements help awaken energy and bring your presence into the body. These movements are especially supportive after meditation, bringing your awareness from the energetic into the physical.

Opening

After awakening awareness through presence, breath, and visualization, you come to the next layer of pelvic care. These opening practices are nurturing and foundational, supporting warmth and flow in the body.

I've worked with many women using these practices, and I've witnessed profound shifts in both emotional well-being and physical healing. As with everything I share, I offer only what I've found to be deeply supportive and transformative.

Breast Massage

This gentle, accessible practice is a beautiful way to awaken your feminine heart and its connection with the womb. It also supports lymphatic flow, hormone balance, and a sense of nurturing self-touch.

Begin with a small amount of oil. I recommend organic jojoba oil or rose oil if you wish to bring in additional loving energy. Massage around your breasts, nipples, and outward toward your underarms (remember, breast tissue extends farther than you think). Use light, intuitive strokes.

Even just five minutes of loving touch can be deeply nourishing. As you massage, breathe, smile, and let your hands become warm with healing energy. As always, this is not about technique, it's about attention and the simple act of touch.

Herbal Pelvic Steaming

Herbal pelvic steaming, also called vaginal steaming, is a healing practice for women in all stages of life.

This practice involves a woman sitting over a bowl of hot steamy water steeped in medicinal herbs. It promotes health and healing of not just the external genitalia, but also by stimulating the cervix, affects the reproductive, hormonal, and nervous systems.

This practice supports uterine cleansing, soothes pelvic tissues, and holds a wide range of healing properties depending on the herbs used. It can assist with regulating menstrual cycles, preparing the womb for conception, and supporting postpartum recovery.

Pelvic steaming is also healing alongside other modalities for those with deeper reproductive imbalances. I have seen it to be helpful for those experiencing endometriosis, fibroids, cervical dysplasia, and chronic pelvic pain. In those situations, it's best used alongside other holistic modalities such as abdominal massage, castor oil packs, emotional healing, and making diet and lifestyle changes.

For women in their bleeding years, steaming offers deep support for reproductive vitality. During the postpartum time, it helps reduce swelling and soothe tender tissues. In perimenopause and menopause, it supports the gentle release of what may have accumulated emotionally and physically over a lifetime.

One of the most beautiful aspects of this practice is its capacity for emotional healing, particularly for trauma stored in the pelvis. Steaming helps reprogram patterns of disconnection and numbness into states of safety, pleasure, and self-love.

In the Maya tradition, herbal steaming is known as *bajos* and has been used for generations by midwives and wise women to restore reproductive health. Dr. Rosita Arvigo, DN, brought this practice to the West through her work with the Arvigo® Techniques of Maya Abdominal Therapy. She apprenticed for over 13 years with renowned Belizean medicine man Don Elijio and midwife Miss Hortense to learn their traditional wisdom and lifeways [1].

While many associate the practice with Central America, versions of pelvic steaming exist all over the world. Keli Garza, founder of Steamy Chick and one of the most active educators on this practice, has compiled hundreds of case studies and even conducted clinical research showing the benefits of postpartum steaming. She's documented steaming traditions across Africa,

Asia, and the Americas, showing that this is not fringe or new age, but ancestral wisdom [2].

Overall, steaming supports warmth, circulation, and healing. Even in the absence of symptoms, most women carry some amount of pelvic stagnation due to a modern sedentary lifestyle. I've also found steaming to deeply relax the pelvic floor muscles, enhancing sensation and pleasure.

The warm steam softens tissues, but the deeper healing comes from the plants themselves. Each herb offers unique properties: some stimulate circulation, others soothe inflammation, and many offer emotional or energetic support as well.

You can use fresh or dried herbs but never use essential oils in your steam. They're too concentrated and don't offer the entire plant's medicine.

There are many ways to choose herbs. You can follow your intuition, buy ready-made blends, or create your own based on what you're working with. In the following pages, you'll find a guide to some of my favorite herbs and their physical and energetic benefits.

A note on safety: Because steaming increases pelvic circulation, there are a few situations where it's best to pause or modify:

- Pelvic infections: Wait until the infection has cleared or use very specific antibacterial herbs and steam for 10 minutes.
- During menstrual bleeding: Steam only when you're spotting at the end of your bleed.
- Pregnancy: Avoid until the postpartum period, once all fresh bleeding has stopped.
- Trying to conceive: Avoid steaming after ovulation.
- Heavy or spontaneous bleeding: If you experience irregular or excessive flow, hold off until things are resolved.

Remember, steaming is a supportive ritual, not a replacement for medical care. I trust you to tune in, listen to your body, and seek support when needed. This book offers steaming as a gentle, loving tool to support your vibrant health.

Steaming can be especially helpful when working with long-held trauma or reproductive conditions like endometriosis. Ashley's story offers a powerful example of what this healing can look like.

Ashley's Healing Story

After years of pain, a sudden rupture sent Ashley into emergency surgery. A tumor had twisted her left ovary. It was only after the ovary was removed that they confirmed she had severe endometriosis.

And yet, she conceived. But after that birth, she experienced a uterine prolapse. The practitioners she turned to weren't able to offer real help. But Ashley had deep faith in the healing power of her body.

She found pelvic steaming, and after two months, her prolapse resolved. In five months, her endometriosis cleared. What came through her womb was thick, black, web-like tissue—years of stagnation, grief and pain releasing through the steam. She went from being bedridden to experiencing the first pain-free menstrual cycle of her life.

After this miracle-level healing, she became a pelvic steaming and somatic practitioner herself.

While there's a clear physical mechanism to how steaming promotes pelvic circulation and tissue release, Ashley speaks to something vital that lies beneath that.

"There's a nervous system component. Steam is a catalyst for emotional repair and healing. Women would come in shut down, then things would start to shift. Sometimes they

would cry, be angry, sleepy, people have such a variety of reactions."

She talks about how sexual abuse memories began to surface when she started steaming, and how this practice helped her move and release these memories. She told me she's never seen a woman with endometriosis or fibroids who doesn't also carry a history of sexual trauma.

Steaming is a gentle way to come back to the body, especially when it hasn't felt safe to be there. The warmth, the plants, allow a woman to experience the healing power of simply receiving. It's a way to feel something good in the body again, a felt sense of safety.

As you can see, steaming clears more than just physical tissue. It helps move emotion and stored imprints. In the next section, you'll learn how to create your own ritual at home.

Creating a Pelvic Steaming Ritual

Whether you're harvesting your own plants or using dried herbs, begin by holding them with gratitude and saying a prayer or intention. Bring a large pot of water to a boil, add about ½ cup of fresh herbs or ¼ cup of dried herbs, and cover the pot with a lid and simmer for 10 minutes.

When you're ready, remove the lid and place the pot beneath a steaming stool or on the ground with a towel underneath the pot. Then, find a way to kneel or squat safely above the steam.

Drape a blanket around your waist to hold the warmth in. The steam should feel soothing, never too hot. If you're squatting or on all fours, shift your position slightly as needed to stay comfortable and allow the heat to circulate.

Use this time to breathe, meditate, and send love to your pelvic bowl. Let the warmth melt tension. Stay here for about 20–25 minutes.

After steaming, wrap yourself in something warm, lie down, and rest. You may feel relaxed or even sleepy.

In the following images, you'll see different positions and setups you can try.

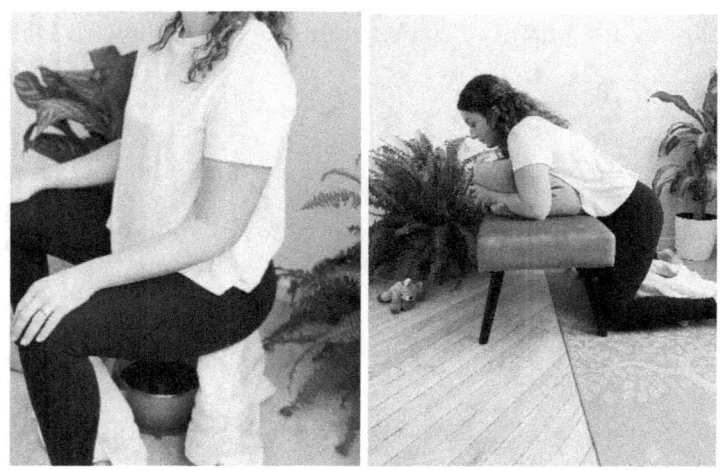

Photos of possible pelvic steaming positions. Source: Kyleigh James.

Herbs for Pelvic Steaming

The healing power of steaming comes not just from the warmth, but from the medicine in the plants.

In the next few pages, some favorite herbs for pelvic steaming are detailed. Each one offers unique support for your body and spirit. If a plant is edible, it's likely also safe to use in a steam. Let your intuition guide you.

Basil (Ocimum basilicum)

This beloved kitchen herb carries powerful medicine. In a steam, basil stimulates blood flow, supports fluid movement, and soothes menstrual cramps. It's also antimicrobial and cleansing.

Basil also has a rich history of magical properties and has been connected to fertility. It has been used to deflect negative energy while attracting prosperity and peace. In Ayurveda, Holy Basil, or Tulsi, is revered as an adaptogen. Add Tulsi to your steam if you're feeling depleted. This is a plant to call on when you're seeking grace and strength.

Calendula/Marigold (Calendula officinalis)

A flower of pure sunshine. Calendula is a gentle healer: anti-inflammatory, antibacterial, and soothing to irritated tissue. It's perfect for postpartum healing, vaginal tears, pelvic pain, or scar tissue.

Energetically, calendula uplifts the spirit and brings softness and joy. It helps restore self-love to places that feel forgotten. Let it remind you of your inherent light.

Damiana (Turnera diffusa)

Damiana is known as an aphrodisiac and promotes deep relaxation. It also improves mood and overall well-being.

Steam with damiana when reconnecting to your libido, sacral chakra, or sensual self. Damiana centers you deeply to your root.

Oregano (Origanum vulgare)

A strong circulatory stimulant, oregano is cleansing and warming. Use it sparingly in your blends; a little goes a long way.

Oregano means "joy of the mountains" in Greek, and its lore includes blessings for weddings and vitality. Steam with oregano to invoke love and the joy of life.

Lavender (Lavandula angustifolia)

This is a wonderful flower to add to any herbal blend. Lavender is antibacterial/microbial and deeply calming to the body-mind. It also promotes menstrual flow and eases cramping.

Spiritually, lavender is a soothing balm for the nervous system and creative center. Use it to de-stress or support transitions like perimenopause.

Lemon Balm (Melissa officinalis)

A subtle mood-lifter, lemon balm eases anxiety and tension. It also relieves PMS symptoms and supports emotional flow. Use lemon balm in blends when you're calling in joy and calm.

Motherwort (Leonurus cardiaca)

This is the plant of the Great Mother. It invokes protection, openness, peace, and deep surrender. On a physical level, it tones and cleanses the uterus. Motherwort is especially nurturing for mothers, postpartum healing, or pregnancy loss. It teaches us how to mother ourselves while feeling safely held.

Mugwort (Artemisia vulgaris)

Mugwort is steeped in ancient magic and healing. It balances hormones, relieves cramping, and helps stimulate a sluggish or painful period.

Spiritually, mugwort is a dream activator, supporting visioning. Use when you are seeking more guidance, magic, and creative (and literal) flow in your life.

Raspberry leaf (Rubus idaeus)

A beloved uterine tonic, raspberry leaf strengthens and tones the uterus and pelvic muscles while also relaxing them.

It's wonderful for postpartum healing, heavy periods, and overall female wellness. Energetically, raspberry leaf is a plant of pure sunshine and teaches boundaries—think of the sweetness of the fruit, and the thorns that protect it. Drink as a tea while you steam for added nourishment and grounding.

Rose (Rosa)

Rose is a classic womb and heart medicine, reminding you to balance your softness with boundaries.

Astringent and cooling, rose petals support tissues after birth or heavy bleeding and soothes inflammation. It is also supportive during menopause when cooling and nourishment is needed.

Yarrow (Achillea millefolium)

Yarrow is a powerful healer for the blood and womb. It regulates flow and supports circulation and cleansing.

Yarrow supports during menopause and ovarian cyst healing. Its qualities are astringent, tonifying, cleansing, and anti-bacterial.

Yarrow is one of the oldest medicinal plants with a rich history of use. It has been considered a deeply protective and spiritual plant.

Witch Hazel (Hammamelis virginiana)

Witch hazel is cooling and astringent, which is great for healing swollen tissues, hemorrhoids, and postpartum inflammation.

Only use the plant (leaves and bark), not store-bought witch hazel extract. Spiritually, it's a guide plant, helping you locate truth in unseen places.

Pelvic Steaming Protocol Suggestions

Below are suggested protocols for different seasons and needs. As always, tune into your body and adapt based on what feels best.

All-Purpose Healing

For general wellness and flow support, steam once the week before your period, and again on the last day of your period, as long as the blood is brown or just spotting. Always wait until fresh red blood has fully passed.

Fertility

Steaming can be a powerful way to support fertility by helping cleanse and nourish the uterine lining.

- Begin at least 3 months before trying to conceive.

- Steam once before your period and again after your period ends (1-3 times), up until ovulation.
- Avoid steaming after ovulation if actively trying to conceive—let the potential "nest" rest.

Supportive herbs: lavender, calendula, rose petals, basil.

Painful or Irregular Periods

When periods are painful or irregular, steaming can ease pelvic congestion and help restore balance. But true healing also includes rest, nourishment, and lifestyle shifts during your bleeding time.

- Steam 2-3 times the week before your period.
- Steam again once at the end of your period, when spotting begins.

Supportive herbs: motherwort, mugwort, calendula, chamomile, oregano, basil.

Postpartum

Postpartum is one of the best times to begin a steaming practice. It supports uterine cleansing, healing of sore or swollen tissues, and emotional integration. Keeping new mothers warm is an essential part of traditional cultures all around the world.

- Begin after fresh bleeding has stopped (or sooner if your intuition guides you).
- Steam daily or every other day for about a month, or as long as you feel called. Sessions can be shorter, about 10 minutes.

Supportive herbs: raspberry leaf, calendula, chamomile, witch hazel, comfrey, oatstraw, motherwort, yarrow.

Miscarriage and Abortion

Pregnancy loss is a postpartum experience, one that is often not respected by our culture or even ourselves. There are many layers of emotional and spiritual healing to work through, and steaming can help reconnect a woman to her center during this time. If there are any signs of infection, see a medical provider.

- If tissue remains but no infection is present, steaming may help gently move it out.
- Once bleeding stops, continue steaming through the next few months (see all-purpose healing suggestion) to support cycle regulation.

Supportive herbs: calendula, lavender, mugwort, motherwort, oregano, rose petals.

Perimenopause and Menopause

Steaming during this passage can help restore juiciness, maintain connection to your womb, and release anything energetically held in the uterus.

- You can steam even after bleeding has stopped. Many women experience a gentle release years later. You may wish to align this with the moon cycle, steaming on the new or full moon.

- Use this practice to maintain connection to your root and support pelvic vitality.

Supportive herbs: raspberry leaf, mugwort, oregano, chamomile, damiana.

Emotional Healing

Pelvic steaming is nourishing on an emotional and spiritual level, especially after experiencing trauma. It can help transmute patterns of numbness, fear, or disconnection into pleasure and self-love.

This is a potent time to meditate during your steam and offer yourself compassion and loving energy. Remind yourself that you are worthy of receiving pleasure and goodness.

Supportive herbs: rose, lavender, lemon balm, motherwort, calendula.

Castor Oil Packs

Castor oil packs are a great practice for circulation, healing, and nervous system nourishment.

Castor oil comes from a plant known as Palma Cristi, or "Hand of Christ," and is sometimes called the Wonder Tree. It's long been revered as a sacred, deeply healing medicine [3].

Use wherever there is a need for flow, softening, or healing. Castor oil is particularly supportive for the womb and sacral area, especially in cases of scar tissue, pelvic pain or numbness, lower back or SI joint pain, or emotional traumas.

Over the sacrum, castor oil softens adhesions, reduces inflammation, and brings circulation to pelvic nerves. This can increase sensation and pleasure within the pelvic floor. When properly absorbed into the bloodstream, feel-good hormones are released, and the parasympathetic nervous system is activated for deep rest. Try using packs on both the womb and sacral area and see how each one benefits you.

Castor oil packs are generally safe for most people. However, take care in the following situations:

- Pregnancy: Let the "nest" rest. This is a great healing practice after birth, especially after a cesarean.
- Pelvic Mesh: Avoid packs over surgical mesh. These implants are designed to embed into tissues and cannot be fully removed. Increasing circulation in the area may cause unwanted migration or issues. Instead, use energy healing or visualization: imagine the mesh dissolving into radiant light, or surround it with healing protection to bless it as it does its job.
- Cancer or Active Infections: Always consult a trusted practitioner

What You'll Need:

- Organic, cold-pressed, extra virgin, hexane-free castor oil (in a glass bottle)
- Wool or cotton flannel, piece cut to size
- Optional: castor oil wrap product
- Optional: heating pad or hot water bottle
- Small bowl
- 1 wet washcloth (for cleanup) + 1 dry washcloth (to protect items from oil stains)

How to Begin:

1. Cut a piece of flannel to fit over the womb or sacral area.
2. Soak the cloth in castor oil (saturated but not dripping).
3. For a womb pack:
    a. Lie on your back, place the cloth directly on the skin.
    b. Cover with a dry washcloth, then heating pad (if using), and finally a blanket tucked around your hips for compression.
4. For a sacral pack:

    a. Put down a heating pad, then a dry washcloth on top.

    b. Put the castor oil pack directly over your sacrum, then lay down so the oil cloth only touches the washcloth, and you can feel the soothing heat behind it.

5. Use the wet washcloth to wipe your hands or skin.
6. Rest for 30–45 minutes. Breathe deeply, relax, and meditate on receiving warmth and healing.

A suggested rhythm is to use 3 times per week, every other day. Continue for 3 weeks per menstrual cycle, skipping during your bleed. Try 3 full cycles, then take a 1-month break. Reassess if more cleansing or flow support is needed. You can always do monthly or seasonally as desired.

A Healing Story

A woman came to me with very painful periods from endometriosis. More than half her month was spent in pain. She had already booked her hysterectomy but gave it about a month and saw me first. She held out hope that maybe I could help.

She had been trying for some time for her second child, but she couldn't wait much longer. She massaged her belly and womb every day and did castor oil packs a few times per week. She especially loved the packs; she had many distinct memories of her grandmother using castor oil. Two cycles later, she was pregnant. When I held my hands over her womb, I felt the presence of her angels surrounding her.

Alchemy

Within this section, you enter the heart of pelvic awakening, when you bring your healing hands to your most sacred feminine spaces. This is about more than just learning techniques; it's about embodiment and healing through loving presence.

Ideally, massage is learned in person, or through video. That's why this section offers an overview for reference and then links to guided video instruction.

I was trained as a massage therapist, where much emphasis is placed on legitimacy and technique. And also, massage is a healing art. Every time you touch someone, you enter their energetic field. When you touch yourself, especially your abdomen and internal pelvic floor, you contact a potential realm of emotions and memories.

Chapter 5 was an exploration of trauma and somatic healing. Know that this work can be activating. That's why I emphasize a gentle and slow approach. Above all, follow your body.

Abdominal and Womb Massage

This is one of the most supportive practices you can do for physical health and vitality.

Massaging the abdomen increases circulation, clears congestion, stimulates lymph and nerve function, and promotes the body's innate ability to self-heal. It's particularly helpful for cycle-regulation, supporting fertility, and postpartum recovery. It's also a grounding practice of self-love and connection.

Whether you're feeling well already or working through digestive or reproductive imbalances, this is a deeply centering practice. Most women attest to feeling happier, lighter, and simultaneously more grounded after doing this massage.

To help you get started, I've included a link to a guided video in the *Pelvic Awakening Bonus* section at the end of this book. You'll need to go to that webpage and enter your email address, then a link will be sent to you. This is the same intuitive, heart-centered routine I shared with women in my private sessions.

You can begin with a castor oil pack to soften tissues and awaken flow. Always empty your bladder first and lie with a supportive pillow under your knees. If you have a prolapse, also elevate your hips slightly.

The routine usually takes around 10 minutes, though the video is 35 minutes for demonstration. At first, watch and follow along until everything feels familiar. After that, feel free to do it on your own and in your own way. You don't have to follow it exactly, use any touch that feels intuitive. However, this is a great framework in which to start.

Use this time as an opportunity to reconnect to your center. Be present with your body and its sensations. I always tell women to bring their full awareness wherever their hands are.

There are some situations to be cautious:

- Pelvic Mesh: Use only visualization or energy work.
- IUD: Avoid direct womb massage; upper abdomen is okay.
- Pregnancy: Light, intuitive upper abdominal massage is safe (at least to the top of the fundus as it grows upwards); avoid pressure on the womb
- Postpartum: Begin when you feel ready; after C-section, wait 6–8 weeks until the scar is fully healed. Most women that have given birth have some degree of abdominal muscle separation, so adapt the upper portion of the massage accordingly.
- Infections or Cancer: Avoid until resolved or talk to your health care provider.
- Hernias: Avoid direct pressure over the site.

- Menstruation: Take a break or use feather-light touch. Let the womb rest and allow the natural downward energy to flow.

You can do this massage daily when not bleeding. Deep, slow, and intentional is the way, with soft, relaxed hands.

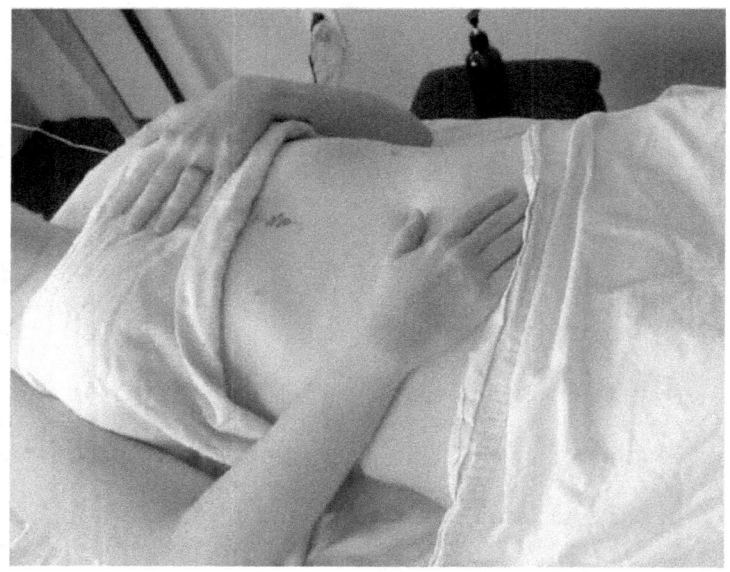

Photo of womb-heart meditation. Source: Author.

Abdominal and Womb Massage Routine

Warm-Up

- Begin with a minute or two of loving presence with your body, centering in the heart and womb.
- Start with large, clockwise warm-up strokes over the abdomen, following the natural flow of the intestines.
- Gradually make the circles smaller and move into deeper pressure as your tissues soften and open.
- Massage along the front, sides, and back of your ribs, creating spaciousness in the diaphragm.

Lower Abdominal Area

- Over the ovaries, massage very gentle circles to wake up the area.
- After locating the pubic bone and hip bones (ASIS) as your landmarks, move into the deeper lower abdominal techniques:

- Scoop upward along the midline from the pubic bone toward the navel, sinking deeply into the tissue. Repeat three times.
- Use the sides of your pinkies to scoop in from hip bone toward the midline, supporting with the opposite hand for deeper pressure.
- Complete the right side three times, then the left side three times.
- Repeat the full sequence (center, right, left) for three rounds total.

Upper Abdominal Area

- Warm up the solar plexus area with circles to awaken and soften this area.
- If you have not been pregnant or do not have an abdominal muscle separation (diastasis recti):
    - Place your hands flat beneath the ribs, fingertips meeting in the center. Sink in deeply and slowly scoop downward toward the navel. Repeat three times.

- If you have experienced pregnancy or have abdominal muscle separation:
    - Keep fingertips apart, find the edges of the separation, and use a weaving together motion downward, ending at the navel.
    - You may also use the base of your palms or a crisscrossing technique down the midline.
    - Repeat three times down the midline.
- Using fists, move diagonally from beneath the ribs toward the navel. Use the other hand to support deep pressure.
- Complete the right side three times, then the left side three times.
- Repeat the full sequence (center, right, left) for three rounds total.

Deep Navel Work

- About an inch outward from the navel, sink in with your fingertips and create deep, slow circles around the entire navel.
- Move clockwise, pausing over any areas of tension or tenderness until you feel a softening or shift.

Closing

- End with big circles over the entire abdomen. Send gratitude and love into your body.

Pelvic Floor Massage

This is the most intimate and potentially transformational work in this chapter. The pelvic floor holds your stories, and ultimately your vitality.

Many women feel a lack of sensation in their pelvic floor that stems from a deep disconnection. This happens due to shame, trauma, or the cultural norm of disembodiment.

You may also believe on some level that this disconnection will keep you safe. If you can limit connection, then you don't have to feel the grief, the pain, and memories that may be stored there. *But it's still there*. In limiting connection, you also shut out your full pleasure and sexual expression. This affects your wild feminine spirit.

When there's compassionate touch with no agenda, it can be deeply healing. Most women have only experienced genital touch from medical providers or sexual partners (that likely lacked reverence). Perhaps there were traumatic experiences. So, before you begin, tune in. Ask your body if it's a yes. If it's no, honor that. Pushing past your no only continues to program you in ways that create more armoring and numbness. Listening to your inner voice is more healing than the massage itself.

Understanding Pelvic Tension

Pelvic floor massage is healing enough on this emotional and energetic level, but it also carries numerous physical benefits as well. This practice improves muscular strength and vitality, promotes increased sensation, and reduces deep tension.

Tension is often mistaken for strength. But a chronically tense pelvic floor is like a stretched rubber band—weakened, fragile. You can also have a tense pelvic floor even if you feel it is too "lax", especially after giving birth. True strength is supple and responsive: able to fully engage and fully release.

To have a healthy and vibrant pelvic floor, you need regular movement, daily awareness, intuitive massage, and breath. This work supports blood flow, lymph movement, and awakening nerve pathways. By freeing up restrictions in fascia, ligaments, and other tissues, releasing trigger points and tense muscles, and deepening embodiment, you come to a place of balance and lightness in your pelvic floor over time. Pain tends to result from chronic tension that constricts and inhibits healthy flow within the muscle.

Most people are carrying around pain and tension in their pelvic floor that can be softened with awareness and massage. You don't need to know how to do trigger point or myofascial work on yourself to release tension. Any intuitive touch is healing. Any loving awareness is softening.

When energy starts to flow and tension releases, your body knows what to do to find balance. It has a template for healing and vitality. I've seen this again and again. When tension is released, energy can be re-woven. This may look like:

- Experiencing more joy and a sense of well-being
- Feeling grounded and centered in your body and pelvis
- Increased pleasure and sensitivity
- Awakening creativity

- Healing from acute or chronic reproductive imbalances

Sometimes, though, the tension is deeper than muscle or tissue. Sometimes it's a holding pattern that's been there for years. This is protective and unconscious.

The concept of "de-armoring" can be a helpful lens for self-healing. It comes from the work of Wilhelm Reich, a psychoanalyst and somatic therapist of the 1930s. He theorized that our psychological coping patterns manifest as physical tension or "armor" in the body. This armor can interfere with the natural flow of energy and show up as numbness, stiffness, pain, or disconnection.

Reich identified seven "armor segments" throughout the body, and the seventh is the pelvic segment, including the pelvis and lower limbs. He believed that we needed to release the upper segments first to fully unlock the pelvis.

Similarly, in Chi Nei Tsang (a Taoist form of abdominal massage), the belly must be massaged before the genitals are worked with. Sometimes the trauma in the pelvis is too much, and you must go slowly. That's why I always recommend starting with meditation, breast massage, and then abdominal and womb massage before working with the internal pelvic area.

Internal Massage Practice

If you have scar tissue or particularly tense pelvic floor muscles, I suggest using castor oil. Otherwise, jojoba oil is my favorite.

Create a dark, quiet space. Take time to breathe. Begin with breast massage and then abdominal massage. This helps awaken a presence in the body and helps ease you into deeper layers of touch.

Avoid penetrating right away. Your tissues need time to soften and fully expand, which takes at least 15–20 minutes. If emotions come up, sit with them for awhile, move into another practice, or simply take a break.

When you feel ready, pause with your hand on your vulva. If you receive a clear yes, you can begin in a purely intuitive way or use a framework for exploration.

Just like the abdominal massage practice, bring your awareness to wherever you are touching. You can start by inserting one finger, and sitting with the sensations for some time, allowing the tissue around your finger to soften. Notice the terrain, all the ridges and contours, pleasure spots, numb areas, or even painful places. The vagina is a space that is alive with nerves, blood vessels, glands, and energy pathways.

What is the temperature like? Do you feel tension? Do you feel any emotions? This is a time to sit with simply noticing and not trying to change anything.

See how breathing affects tone, and how there is less of a tight hold around your finger as you relax and breathe more fully. You can move deeper and see how the textures and feelings change. Spend some time massaging any areas you feel drawn to.

You can use the "four corner" map for orientation: upper left, upper right, lower left, lower right—squeeze and then fully relax each corner and see how each responds. Does one area squeeze more? Relax less?

When you feel ready for more structure, you can use a simple internal map to guide your awareness.

You can orient by visualizing your internal space as a circle or mandala. Move slowly around the circle, noticing sensations as you go. If you find small nodules or tender points, hold for 30 seconds or more, breathing and noticing any shifts in tone, temperature, or emotion.

Note: Avoid applying pressure directly at the top or bottom of your inner space, where the bladder and rectum lie. These areas are more sensitive and don't need focused or deep touch.

In my work with women, I would find areas that held intense heat, sometimes almost burning, when holding these points. Stay present and breathe through it. These are moments of positive change. When the temperature shifts or tension softens, you'll know something has moved.

At the end of your exploration session, you can go back to each of the four corners and squeeze around your finger again. Do you notice any difference now? Often women find that their squeezes are stronger, and the muscles more fully relax after the squeeze. Everything tends to feel more alive.

This is a powerful awakening practice, bringing in vitality through massage, breath, and the quality of your attention.

Much of this guidance is intentionally left open, because following your own intuition (with some structure) is how you find your unique path to healing.

Cervical Scar Tissue Massage

In Chapter 2, I mentioned some of the experiences and procedures that can lead to scar tissue around the cervix or within the pelvic floor, such as birth, surgery, or trauma. If you feel this may be present for you, begin with the same massage practice in the previous section, with a few additional suggestions.

A wonderful way to start is with an herbal pelvic steam. Choose herbs that are circulation-promoting and soothing. Let this be a grounding warm-up for deeper work.

When you feel ready for internal work, I recommend using castor oil. Castor oil is a traditional remedy for both external and internal scar tissue. It's known to soften hardened tissue and stimulate a gentle immune response. It increases the production of lymphocytes (white blood cells), which play a role in regulating inflammation and wound healing [4]. Wherever there is congestion, reduced blood flow, scar tissue, or stagnation, castor oil can support healing.

After spending some time massaging internally, you can move into touch around the area of your cervix.

Take your time. You may not find your cervix right away. Its texture and position will change depending on where you are in your cycle. It may feel firmer and lower closer to your bleed, and higher and softer around ovulation. When you do find it, gently massage the area. It may feel sensitive, numb, or tense. Simply notice what you feel and never push past discomfort.

Visualize the tissue softening, warming, and increasing circulation. Imagine your loving touch bringing health, energy, and renewal into your pelvic bowl.

Be with this area as long as you like, blending touch, presence, and breath. Go slow.

Deep Pelvic Floor Release

If you carry deep pelvic tension or find areas that are hard to reach, sitting on a tennis ball centered at your perineum can be profoundly helpful. Go very slow at first. Breathe, soften, and allow the tissues to melt. Stay for a few minutes or as long as feels supportive.

Closing + Bringing it into Your Life

This chapter offered a range of practices, each one intended to support healing, connection, and vitality within your female center. You don't need to do everything all at once. In fact, it's often more helpful to start with one or two that feel most meaningful to you right now.

Some women begin with meditation, while others are drawn to pelvic steaming or castor oil packs. Over time, you may find that certain practices feel more supportive during different phases of your cycle or life.

It's about coming into relationship with yourself and having a set of rituals and practices to work with when needed. These practices are meant to be returned to, in different seasons and stages of your life.

Each has a unique role to play in supporting your vibrancy, clarity, and coming home to yourself.

Integration

Physical practices help anchor transformation in the body, creating a felt sense of change. Feel into the subtle or profound shifts, noticing what feels clearer or lighter. Trust that each imprint you clear, each grounded moment of awareness, and each time you honor your body's messages, *is* the healing.

1. What practice within this chapter has been most helpful for you as you've integrated it into your life?

2. After doing any of the practices or meditations so far, what old emotions or stories have begun to move within you?
3. What part of your body feels most ready to explore, and what part still asks for more patience?

7

Fertility and Pregnancy

The Womb Portal

I was doing this for every woman who would ever be born and would ever give birth. Just as they had done it for me and would do it for me, again and again.

THE MADONNA SECRET

Pregnancy and birth are the biggest unfolding and flowering of a woman's creative potential. They forever change the rhythms of her life, as she moves from naturally centering herself to centering her children.

The creative force within the womb is activated during this life passage in a very real way. This book is about the female pelvis and its inherent capacity. This power lives in the pelvis in part because of the uterus and its ability to hold and create life. But it's more than biological, it's also a direct thread to source.

Pregnancy brings a woman into a more open state of being. The pelvic bowl eventually expands to its full capacity as the ligaments that hold it together soften. Emotions flow more freely in response to high levels of sacred hormones, vulnerability, and the beauty and discomforts of this time. This is all part of pregnancy, channeling the codes for new life in each moment. Being open and receptive is part of this.

Just as the physical body opens, the energetic layers mirror this expansion. All energy centers are more open during pregnancy and completely blast open during the altered state of birth. While blocks may form due to personal experience or trauma, this openness is an original template.

Source: Marina Zlochin

This chapter offers support for the passages of preconception and pregnancy. While pelvic wellness and the female system remain the focus, embodied practices and holistic suggestions are shared to nourish you along the way.

Preparing to Conceive

The desire for a child is a very strong pull, and carries a woman through all the ways she'll be continually tested. This desire is the beginning of the motherhood continuum. I believe humans have an instinct to seek initiation; to be unraveled and transformed. This path is made for a woman—if she chooses it, it's her birthright. Each time she carries life, she emerges re-born into the Butterfly Mother.

If you're reading this, this may be the physical and spiritual renewal you're longing for. Women come face to face with the Mystery, led through the portal of life and death in their own bodies. They touch Creation. The pelvis, again, is the site of immense change, as alchemy is its very nature.

Preconception is a liminal time. It's one which requires patience, trust, and the courage to step into the unknown, guided by love. Once you conceive and receive a seed of life, something within you will be birthed, regardless of outcome. This is a sacred commitment. You will not be the same.

Nourishing the Womb

It's optimal to begin preparing for conception at least three months prior. It typically takes 80-90 days for an egg to mature, and the nourishment given to the body during this time can directly affect egg quality.

Deep nourishment and reduced exposure to toxins or environmental chemicals create an ideal environment for conception. And while conception often occurs unplanned, if you're reading this, you're likely approaching pregnancy with intention. When you can prepare, you ensure a better foundation.

In general, the body prioritizes the health of the fetus, often at the mother's expense. Women who conceive while depleted may experience postpartum challenges: fatigue, brittle teeth, pelvic floor issues, or autoimmune symptoms. But pregnancy can be a time of vitality if you support it.

Animal foods have always been considered key fertility foods. Eggs, raw dairy products, meats, organs, and animal-based broths are the most nutrient-dense and bioavailable foods for nourishment. Eating an abundant supply of all of these in the preconception time is great preparation for your physical journey. For further reading on optimal fertility through postpartum nutrition, read *Real Food for Pregnancy* by Lily Nichols.

Vitamin and mineral-rich herbal infusions can also be a great addition to your diet. Steep a small handful of herbs in a large mason jar, pour boiling water over, and let it infuse for at least 4–8 hours. Then drink throughout the next day or two. My favorite base herbs for mothers include raspberry leaf, nettle, alfalfa, and oatstraw. I often add smaller amounts of lemon balm, spearmint, orange peel, and/or rose hips. These infusions are deeply hydrating, and they can be continued throughout pregnancy and nursing for deep replenishment.

Many women feel a stagnation within their abdominal and pelvic areas and would benefit from womb massage, pelvic steaming, and castor oil packs in the few months leading up to conception, as shared in Chapter 6.

Some are drawn to detoxing during this time, but I would offer caution with these approaches. It's generally better to support and strengthen the body's natural cleansing processes, rather than use harsh herbs that deplete. Trust that nourishment is the best preparation.

Herbal Support for Preconception

There are many herbs for working with various conditions and situations that women have. It's outside the scope of this book to support women wanting to conceive who have endometriosis, PCOS, fibroids, etc. There are many herbs and lifestyle changes that will support those greatly. Please see Resources for book suggestions if you're needing deeper healing before conception. The herbs I suggest here are for women who are generally in good health, and support hormonal balance, pelvic circulation, and increasing vitamin and mineral stores.

- Maca Root: This fertility superfood supports hormonal balance and is nourishing to the endocrine system. It's also been traditionally used to support energy and libido. Best used as a powder in smoothies or hot drinks.
- Nettle: You will see nettle leaf promoted all over this book because it is truly a nutrient powerhouse for all stages of a woman's life. Nettle leaf also supports healthy iron levels. Best used in an herbal infusion.
- Red Raspberry Leaf: Another herb that is beneficial for any stage of a woman's life. Not only is it rich in vitamins and minerals, but it also has an affinity for the uterus, supporting blood flow to the pelvic area. Best used in an herbal infusion.
- Royal Jelly: Traditionally used as a fertility tonic, it's rich in vitamins and supports egg quality and hormonal balance. Best taken in a honey-royal jelly blend.

Preconception Rituals

In my work with women before I became a mother, I sat at the holy altar of their womb space. Many times, a woman would come to me to prepare for pregnancy. In each of these sessions, the spirit linked to her would be present. Sometimes it was a faraway connection. Other times, an energy would hover near her, and I would feel the innate joyful spirit of new life. They were always full of excitement.

If this is something you believe in, there are many ways to connect with your spirit baby and create rituals to support this special time.

One ritual is to create a spirit baby altar. You can put any baby items you've collected that are meaningful to you. Art, candles, crystals, and any other objects that relate to this desire for your upcoming pregnancy. It can be a space to meditate and connect with your future child.

As you invite them to you, visualize an energetic spaciousness in your womb and life. Journal to them. Say prayers aloud and in your heart. Ask the Great Mother for blessings for the upcoming journey.

Regeneration and Becoming

Pregnancy is regenerative. It's not an innate state of depletion as it's often depicted, but instead one of overflowing vitality. This shift in perspective can change how you experience it entirely.

Regeneration is the body's innate capacity for renewal. When there's injury or damage, healing begins immediately; this is a normal function of the body. But during pregnancy, the regenerative processes of the body accelerate. The metabolic rate increases, tissue repair quickens, and pregnant women carry an ocean of stem cells. This is one of the most regenerative states known.

And yet this regeneration is more than physical. It's what happens when a woman channels the energy of creation itself. Her body vibrates with a higher intelligence; one that renews at a cellular level.

Being pregnant is like borrowing the creative powers of the universe. A woman becomes a channel for something vast and holy. This creatrix energy moves through her, it *is* her, yet it also comes from something greater.

I've experienced my pregnancies as deeply spiritual times in my life. They've tested and shaped me, helping me cultivate surrender and self-trust.

Many modern women go through this journey with a sense of grief and not everyone can place it. Most pregnancy books focus on negative symptoms and clinical stages of development—no touching the joy, revelation, or the recognition of the rite of passage unfolding. The dominant narrative paints pregnancy as an entirely physical experience, one that's uncomfortable at best and dangerous at worst. But pregnancy is a monumental time for a woman. It is her soul work.

Carrying life changes more than just the arrangement of your organs and the size of your belly. It alters who you are going forward. When you call in your children, you open to a mystical process and become a bridge between here and *out there*.

Your hormonal makeup shifts into an entirely new state, which changes your perception and consciousness.

The weaving of consciousness-shifting hormones, a sense of openness, and physical transformation creates profound change in a woman. It's the sacred design of pregnancy.

At the same time women are continually connected to the cosmos, they're also rooted in the body more than ever. This gives an opportunity for deeper embodiment. Remaining grounded during these months and feeling good will look different for each woman. But within this space is an invitation to heal instinct injury and reconnect to your deep inner voice.

Each of the following sections move through the phases of pregnancy as both physical unfolding and soul-deep evolution.

The First Trimester: Descent + Listening

The beginning of pregnancy is often a deep and necessary cleansing. Each phase of the childbearing continuum prepares you perfectly for the next.

Pregnancy begins with a descent; a shift into the altered state of mother-consciousness. The pelvis becomes a vessel, the womb now embodying the bridge between spirit and matter. This is a potent time to awaken your pelvic voice, as so much energy in your body is directed inward toward your center.

Many women experience symptoms like nausea and deep fatigue that bring them inward. The focus at this time is rest, attunement, survival.

It also may be the beginning of protecting your energetic field as fear and outside opinions come to light. Cultivating a sense of surrender and trust is part of the work of pregnancy that'll come up again and again. Through pregnancy, birth, and mothering, you're called to face what you can control—and the many things that are out of your hands.

Some women connect to the spirit of their babies in the preconception time, while others meet them once they embody. It can be an intense time for many as they adjust to holding two different energies in one body. There's an integration period here.

Another theme that comes up during the first few months is rising grief. Our culture doesn't understand the importance of centering mothers, or of meeting the love and nourishment they need.

One of the physiological aspects of early pregnancy nausea is that if you're bed bound, you simply must gather in support. Pregnancy is a highly receptive time, and you're being invited to get comfortable with receiving.

If you're experiencing pregnancy nausea, does this resonate? Do you feel the desire for support and loving company? Do you feel comfortable asking for and receiving this care?

When you have uncomfortable physical symptoms, lay down somewhere quiet and alone. Listen to what's present. Trace the sensations and sit with them. Notice if any emotions come to your awareness. Every sensation has an origin. Can you follow it and find the emotional core? Each symptom you experience offers messages, and thus opportunities for growth and healing.

As the body descends and opens, herbs can support this time by relaxing the nervous system and easing digestion. It's also helpful to replenish internal reserves, as many women eat less than optimally in these couple of months. Below are a few herbs to support you during the first trimester:

- Ginger: There are numerous studies on the beneficial association between ginger and alleviating nausea. One effective remedy for nausea is a combination of ginger extract and vitamin B6.
- Dandelion: Both the leaf and root support the abundant rise in hormones in the first trimester that the liver must process. Supporting these processes through liver

nourishing herbs like dandelion can be helpful. You can take the leaf as a tincture, or the roasted root as a coffee-replacing tea.

- Peach Leaf: Peach leaf has traditionally been used as a nausea and morning sickness remedy. Peach is from the rose family, which offers similar energetic heart medicine. Use in extract form and combine with ginger for even more effectiveness.
- Oatstraw: This offers a wonderful source of minerals (particularly calcium and magnesium), and provides additional support for irritability, fatigue, and stress. Drink as an herbal infusion and combine with nettle leaf for deeper nourishment.

The first trimester is an internal time. In this descent, you return to the body and begin to truly listen.

The Second Trimester: Expansion + Vitality

As the weeks pass, a shift begins. For many women, the second trimester brings relief from the challenges of early pregnancy: a gradual return to energy, appetite, and a sense of self. A fog lifts, and there's light and clarity. It's like emerging from hibernation. At this time, the placenta takes over progesterone production, and there's a completion to the most delicate phases of fetal development that take so much energy from the body.

If you're starting to feel better (and to be clear, it's not everyone), it's a time of rejoicing. It's a time of doing, gathering, and dreaming. What's your intention and vision for the rest of your pregnancy? Your birth? Postpartum? Do you want to take a trip during this energizing time?

As your energy returns, this is also a time to nourish yourself as your appetite usually returns. Supporting blood volume expansion is key for vitality in the months ahead. Prioritize blood-building foods: iron-rich, protein-rich, and mineral-dense, to fuel the body's growth.

The pelvic bowl begins to bloom, creating spaciousness, and the baby's first movements are a call to joyful embodiment. This is a beautiful time to begin herbal body oiling: a daily ritual that brings connection to your expanding center.

Herbal body oiling is deeply calming to the nervous system and supports full-body health. This should be a simple and intuitive ritual, where you massage wherever you feel is needed. Fill a small jar with herbs like calendula, rose, or lavender, then cover completely with jojoba oil. Shake every few days and let infuse for a moon cycle. Strain and store in a cool, dark place.

First-time mothers often find themselves in a liminal place. Not quite maidens, not yet mothers. *Who are you, and who are you becoming?*

While pregnancy is a time for centering yourself, I also encourage women who are pregnant for the first time to surround themselves with mothers in the spirit of service. This is the last time you'll have this freedom to serve and learn. Can you bring a meal and play with her children? Wash her dishes and listen to her?

Today, many women navigate this rite of passage alone or only with other young mothers to be with them. They cook for each other with babies on their hips. Drop off postpartum meals across town with their toddlers.

This isn't entirely how it should be. Maidens and elders in freer phases of life have the opportunity to return to service. This is how we rebuild a mother-centered culture.

The Third Trimester: Deepening + Surrender

Slowly, energy spirals in again, back to center.

The end of pregnancy is a time of fullness. After many moons of swirling in the increasing hormonal matrix of pregnancy, you can start to feel the deeper shifts in consciousness. You might feel altered. Birth is like a vortex, coming closer to bring you into its transformative spiral, and the wisest thing is to be in an altered state of consciousness for this ceremony. It is a slow descent into one's most primal self.

A woman naturally settles, gathers, nests, and prepares for the birth of her baby. She may need to process fear or anxiety of her upcoming birth. Things begin to feel more real. Her emotions are full and asking to be felt and processed. Each time I entered the third trimester, I noticed myself deepening and witnessed how my attention had changed. You would be wise to let yourself walk into this natural space, for it is an important next step to allow the surrender needed for birth and mothering.

As fears and anxieties may get stronger, it becomes the true fire walk of women to process these emotions. How can you find the inner strength to calm yourself; how can you midwife yourself through your fears? The end of pregnancy offers practice before entering birth.

Culturally, we're often encouraged to speak about this time as uncomfortable and inconvenient, to frame pregnancy as something to get through. It's good to be honest about what you're feeling, but if you focus mostly on what's hard, you shape your experience and bypass the potential gifts hidden within discomfort. One thing you can do is turn toward your body with curiosity. What is this sensation telling you? How is this discomfort *preparing* you for birth, for mothering? How can you do the work of cultivating gratitude and strength in the swirling midst of discomfort, even pain?

A woman's oxytocin receptors in her cervix will be highest at the end of pregnancy. This is not just what facilitates labor itself but also part of what causes profound emotional and mental shifts. Mothers who have been through the birth process before have more of these receptors.

During the third trimester, hormones are at their highest levels. Estrogen and progesterone peak around 32 weeks, and blood volume expansion has mostly reached its maximum around this time, plateauing until birth. Prolactin slowly increases throughout the pregnancy, preparing for breastfeeding. Oxytocin, the hormone of love, bonding, and pleasure, also increases steadily. It reaches its highest point during labor and birth, where it helps facilitate strong and efficient uterine contractions.

The pelvic bowl, too, begins to soften. Its tissues and ligaments loosen to prepare for birth, creating a sense of spaciousness and vulnerability. Everything begins to open; it's the body's preparation for the passage ahead.

As you prepare for birth, return to your spirit baby altar. Perhaps you've kept it alive during these months and transformed it into a pregnancy and birth altar. If you're planning a home birth, decorate this space for labor. This may not be where you give birth; above all, it's a space for you during pregnancy. Come here daily and meditate on your ideal birth vision. Bring your fears and prayers. This is where you can gather strength from creating ritual and connect to all the women who came before you.

Pregnancy as Soul Work

This chapter isn't meant to prescribe a way of preparing or moving through pregnancy. It is an invitation to awaken your mother-power. To see pregnancy as a mind-body-spirit journey.

To walk this path well requires a focus on self-nourishment. To protect the sensitive field around you and root your choices in what feels aligned. This is the heart of sovereignty: learning to trust your own knowing more than the noise outside of you.

Pregnancy is personal soul work, but at its very nature, it's also beyond you. You are the soil for the seeds of the future. You're co-creating this story and experience with your child.

The journey of pregnancy is one path of pelvic awakening, but not the only one. The same energies of expansion and transformation live in every woman.

Through pregnancy, the mother line is stirred. It brings forward everything that lives in your bones. Let this pregnancy shape and evolve you. You are walking in the well-worn, old path of all mothers before you.

Integration

Let yourself feel the resonance of this chapter in your body. You've entered a new layer of connection with your womb, one of mystery and continual transformation, both body and spirit. Reflect on the self-trust you are building, how it changes the way you move through the world, and let it carry you through this threshold.

1. During your pregnancy or preparation period, what is one ancestral strength you feel guiding you?
2. What inner shifts have you noticed as you move through your pregnancy?

3. Envision and write down your ideal birth vision. What does it look like? How do you feel? Imagine it in detail, from the beginning until the end.

8

Postpartum and Motherhood

Cultivating Vitality

Welcome, the women's voices said. Welcome home.
You are one of us now!

THE MADONNA SECRET

There's an altered state to the postpartum time. It's different from pregnancy, and different from who you were before. Rhythms shift and orient around new life. There's a slowing down, an earth-paced stillness. This is a time of integration, the final stage of the childbearing year where all that has unfolded begins to settle.

Postpartum is a time of love and release. So much must be let go: extra blood, flowing milk, sweat and tears. They all pour out.

The abdominal and pelvic organs begin to return to their original place. A woman stands in-between who she was, and who she will become. Her identity will be re-weaving over the months ahead. A mother is born, and she falls in love. For a while, she is no longer just herself, she is mama-baby, one unified being. Her presence is fully needed.

I've worked with many women in the weeks, months, years after birth, and I see how physical healing can be simple, with the right elements. However, there is still much to integrate, and even if women have lived their lives as a lone wolf, postpartum and motherhood teach her that she needs other people. Then others have deeper healing paths to walk. This chapter offers a map toward healing and vitality during the sacred postpartum time.

Birth Story Resolution

The pelvic bowl holds memory. However your birth unfolded, it's vital to tell your story and be witnessed. Speaking it aloud brings meaning and integration to the experience.

Your birth stories live on within your body, held in your pelvic bowl and heart. Women will remember their birth stories when they are grandmothers, long after other memories fade. If you don't have a friend who can hold space with compassion, write it down. The telling itself is healing. And it'll likely change over time as new recollections surface and deeper layers reveal themselves.

Birth Story Reflections

If you've experienced multiple births, you may want to complete this process for each one, or you can begin with the birth that feels most tender or unfinished. Some women may want to start with their most recent experience, while others feel drawn to a past birth that still feels unresolved.

Don't forget to remember your loss stories—especially your loss stories. Abortions, miscarriages, stillbirths, early births of any kind. They are births, and the memory lives within you, waiting to be seen and loved.

Begin by writing your birth story in full, especially remembering the moments that feel pivotal. Once you've written it out, reflect on the following questions.

- What is the strongest image or moment that returns to you again and again?
- What do you feel was the role your baby played in this birth experience?
- What did you hope your birth would bring you? What was the medicine it actually brought you?
- If you could re-write your story, what would happen?

Foundations of Postpartum Wellness

Preparing for the postpartum time is among the most important work you can do during pregnancy. Even if you have a beautiful birth, without support you will carry imprints of trauma and struggle to heal and integrate.

Healing after birth begins with rest. It's through deep rest that you support your body's innate intelligence to repair and return to vitality.

Support and rest aren't optional. These are basic needs of a new mother, and in prioritizing these, she sets the foundation for lifelong wellness. Being in bed and having nourishing food brought to her creates the container for recovery. The body will generally heal beautifully when given this time and space. And eating enough calories and protein, especially warm and nourishing meals, provides the building blocks for tissue repair and milk production.

Having a plan in place so that you are able to rest and be fed is crucial, especially if you have other children. Who can you call on for support, so you and your children are tended to in those early weeks? Your only job should be to nap, nurse, eat, and fall in love with your baby. *The Fourth Trimester* by Kimberly Ann Johnson is a great resource for building your practical support web.

Your bleeding will serve as a barometer for how well you're resting and if you're re-entering the world too soon. Increased flow likely signals that you've pushed too fast: getting up to do dishes, running after older children, or diving back into busy activity. The amount of slowness needed varies for each woman, and often it's more than we expect. Some of the pull to re-engage is instinctual, and some comes from a culture that never rests. There are easeful ways to feel connected again while still moving slow—like sitting in a lounge chair in the sun while your children play nearby.

Rest and nourishment are the roots. Everything else flows from there.

After-Birth Yoni Care

If there was tearing or a surgical cut during birth, the most essential support is, again, rest. Often, committing to staying in bed is enough to heal minor tears and can significantly aid recovery from deeper tears or incisions.

A perineal spray or flower hydrosol (amagnificientstory.com is a great resource for garden-grown, mother-created hydrosols) can be soothing when going to the bathroom, helping with swelling, aches, and the stinging that accompanies healing wounds. For tears that need extra care, raw aloe, manuka honey, or propolis spray may offer additional support. Each contains medicinal compounds known for promoting tissue repair. Apply gently and frequently throughout the day until healing is complete.

Herbal pelvic steaming is an ancient way to soothe tissues, reduce inflammation, and support healing. It's best to wait until the heaviest bleeding has passed and any stitches are removed. If you prefer a sitz bath, the same herbs can be used in a warm soak. A simple and effective blend includes yarrow, calendula, rose petals, and Epsom salt.

Longer-term healing is also supported through internal nourishment. Prioritize vitamin C-rich foods and those high in protein and collagen to provide your body with the nutrients it needs for tissue repair and regeneration.

Belly Wrapping

Belly wrapping is a traditional practice used across cultures to support both the physical and energetic reweaving of the abdomen and womb after birth. During pregnancy, the abdominal muscles separate, organs shift, and the body opens in profound ways. While your body knows exactly how to come back together again, gentle support through wrapping can help guide this process, and simply feels good.

You can begin with any long, woven wrap or scarf. Wrapping should support the body by lifting upward, not putting pressure downward onto the pelvic floor.

To begin, lie on your back with knees bent and feet flat. Lift your hips and begin tying from this position, starting around the level of your uterus and wrapping up just beneath the ribs.

Follow your intuition and wear it during the times when your body craves that sense of holding. Belly wrapping not only supports the physical healing of abdominal tissues but also offers energetic closure.

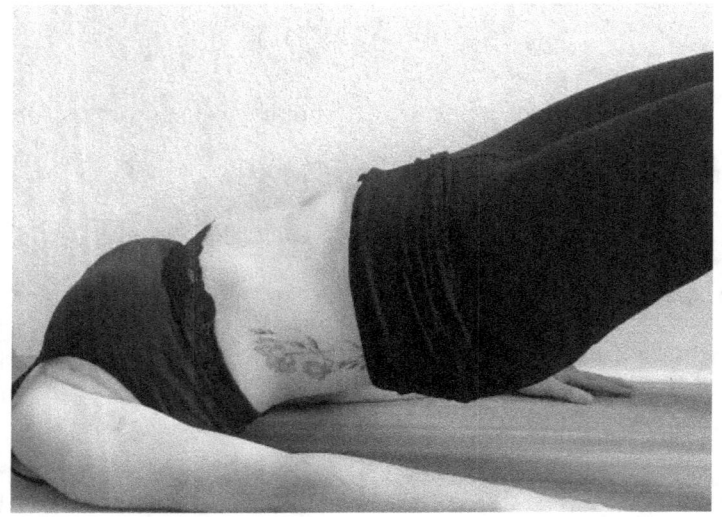

Position for tying a belly wrap. Source: Author.

When Deeper Healing is Needed

Sometimes, healing takes longer after birth. These are emotional situations for women as they often blame themselves or their bodies. Healing needs to recognize the unfelt grief, anger, and shame woven into the symptoms. Common postpartum challenges include pelvic organ prolapse, incontinence and pelvic pain. Cesarean recovery also calls for additional support. This section shares holistic practices, but it's also important to reach out to experienced providers when needed. A pelvic floor physical therapist can offer personalized support, including bodywork, exercises, and deeper insight into your specific needs.

Many women live with pelvic pain or heaviness after birth. These sensations can impact your sense of trust and connection to your body. It's often woven together with a traumatic birth. If this is your experience, you're certainly not alone. I've worked with so many women who are surprised to find themselves here. These are layered conditions, not just physical, and they require patience and giving oneself a lot of love and grace.

For more in-depth support, you can refer to book recommendations in the Resources section. Chapter 5 also offers somatic and emotional tools to help move energy and trauma stored in the pelvic bowl.

These symptoms are signs that your body is asking for greater nourishment, rest, and healing support. Gather in whatever support you need.

Pelvic Organ Prolapse

One of the more common experiences after birth is pelvic organ prolapse, when any of the pelvic organs drop from their original position. It may involve just one organ or several, and there are different degrees. Some estimates say around a third of women experience some level of prolapse after birth [1]. If you feel a sensation of heaviness or pressure in the vagina, this is your body speaking. It's asking you to slow down and call in more support.

Many women will notice these symptoms in the days or weeks after birth. I've seen that when women commit to staying in bed in those early days, most of the time symptoms will resolve. Then if you still have some degree of prolapse 3-6 months later, you can focus on getting external support.

Healing is possible. While it takes consistency and care, I've witnessed profound improvement through committed practice and support. A pelvic floor therapist can help you assess your situation and offer specialized guidance. Here are some additional practices to support your healing:

- Belly Wrapping: Especially during bleeding or anytime you're upright for long periods. Ensure you're tying it correctly to lift organs, not create more downward pressure.

- Abdominal and Womb Massage: Encourages pelvic organ alignment and flow.
- Avoid heavy lifting or high-impact movement.
- Focus on diaphragmatic breathing (where each inhale expands your ribcage in 360 directions) instead of belly breathing, which increases downward pressure.
- Healing foods: Prioritize vitamin C-rich foods and protein. Add in bone broth, collagen, and mineral-rich infusions to help rebuild tissue.
- Herbal Pelvic Steaming: Include toning and lifting herbs like red raspberry leaf, mint, and rose.
- Acupuncture and Chinese Herbs: To support Spleen Qi and overall flow.

Many women have shared with me feeling angry, broken, or alone when experiencing pelvic organ prolapse. It's important to feel what's there fully and know these symptoms aren't your "fault."

After birth, you have an opportunity to reclaim greater vitality than before. To rework your life to receive support. I encourage you to explore the helpful book recommendations in the Resources section if you're navigating this path.

Pelvic Pain

Pain in the vulva or yoni is very common, especially after birth or in women with a trauma history. It may come from a long or difficult labor, scar tissue, or unresolved emotional experiences stored in the tissues. Healing this pain is often a multi-layered process: physical and emotional. You might start with pelvic steaming or sitz baths before approaching internally. Here are some supportive practices:

- Self-Love Cultivation Meditation: With hands on vulva and heart, send loving awareness to begin restoring safety and erotic innocence.
- Herbal Pelvic Steaming and Sitz Baths: Use moistening, anti-inflammatory herbs like marshmallow, rose, and grated turmeric. Chamomile, calendula, and plantain are especially soothing.

- Vaginal Massage: Pain asks for titration, where you slowly do a little more each time. This builds the capacity and tolerance of your nervous system. You might only do external massage for some time before you're able to move internally. You can use castor oil to soften and bring movement and circulation to any tissue that feels tense.

Pain is often the body's call for attention. There's no timeline: healing comes, one layer at a time, when you feel ready for it.

Healing After Cesarean Birth

In 2024 in the U.S., 32.4% of all births were by cesarean [2]. I've worked with many women during this often underworld healing journey. There's a huge gap in postpartum support for women who have a surgical birth.

Doctors provide pain relief and basic aftercare instructions, but many women return home shocked and overwhelmed, left to care for a newborn while healing from major surgery. Birth trauma is often unspoken or dismissed, and women are encouraged to move on, feel grateful, and not dwell on what they feel they've lost. But they deserve more care. A birth experience that didn't go according to a woman's heart-vision is a deep grief. They then need support to process and integrate their experience to mother from a place of wholeness.

Surgery creates an impact on the body's tissues, and recovery takes time. Half of the time, cesareans are unplanned. Even when planned, there can be a lot of emotions to process. Yet I've also seen many women feel at peace with what happened.

Any emotion a woman feels is understandable. Her body is wise, and emotions are revealed when she's ready. Part of the healing is remembering that she can trust herself. To know her instincts are intact.

Most women today receive a low-transverse incision (over the womb), in an area rich in blood vessels and nerves. It's preferable aesthetically and shown to lead to better outcomes for the baby, yet this type of cut disrupts deeper layers of fascia and support systems that are essential for pelvic stability. This can result in low back pain, hip or leg discomfort, pelvic floor dysfunction, and numbness or loss of sensation around the scar.

Scars are like icebergs. They're small on the surface, but with layers that extend far beneath. Deeper scar tissue can develop above, below, or around the incision, affecting the pelvic bowl, cervix, and yoni. Nerves may become caught in fascia, creating tension or pulling on an ovary or the uterus. Some women notice this during ovulation or sex, feeling tugging or pain on one side.

With any surgery, scar tissue forms at the site of the wound and tends to spread over time if nothing is done: generally, up to two years afterward. Adhesions accompany scar tissue, which are fibrous bands that glue tissues together, restricting organ movement and potentially affecting fertility or digestion, or limiting movement.

The Energetics of Cesarean Birth

Energetically, a cesarean can feel like an interrupted birth process. The body often holds a lingering sense of incompletion, even if it's not consciously felt. Reconnecting to the womb-heart channel supports healing by allowing loving energy to flow from the heart and nourish the uterus. During a cesarean, this energetic pathway is often disrupted at the incision site. The Womb-Heart Spiral Meditation from Chapter 6 can help restore the connection between these two essential centers.

I suggest to women to spend some time in meditation when their baby is sleeping on their chest. To envision how they wish their birth had happened. Go through each important moment, really feeling yourself there with all your senses. Feel yourself give birth to your baby, and then the placenta, and in this moment you are holding her. The energetic story can be rewritten and the loop complete.

Closing the birth portal is especially meaningful for those who birthed surgically. Your body holds the story, and it longs to return to wholeness. And you absolutely can heal and thrive. You can find this meditation within this chapter.

Scar Tissue Massage for Cesarean Healing

The most effective remedy I've found for physical healing after cesarean is the abdominal and womb massage (see Chapter 6). It reduces scar tissue and adhesions, strengthens pelvic ligaments, improves lymphatic flow, and enhances circulation. It also invites emotional healing.

I've noticed that women often have a complex relationship with their scar. Many avoid touching or even looking here, to avoid feeling and remembering. Offer grace to yourself. Take your time, you'll know when you're ready.

Wait at least 6-8 weeks after surgery, or until the scar is fully closed and free of infection. It's great to begin a massage session with a castor oil pack to soften tissue and promote deeper healing.

A woman can return her tissue not only to what it was, but to a state even more alive and vibrant. This is a story I often share:

A Healing Story

A client had a cesarean with her first baby and began abdominal and womb massage once her incision healed. She practiced self-massage consistently. When she had another planned cesarean a few years later, the same surgeon was astonished to see no visible scarring on her uterus—he said it looked as if she'd never had a cesarean.

While the general abdominal and womb massage video is included as a free bonus with the book, a second, more in-depth video on scar tissue massage is available in the Pelvic Awakening Sacred Practice Bundle. This practice promotes circulation, softening, and reconnection with areas that may feel hardened or tense. While the video was created specifically to support cesarean healing, it will also be helpful for anyone with scar tissue from endometriosis, or after abdominal or pelvic surgeries.

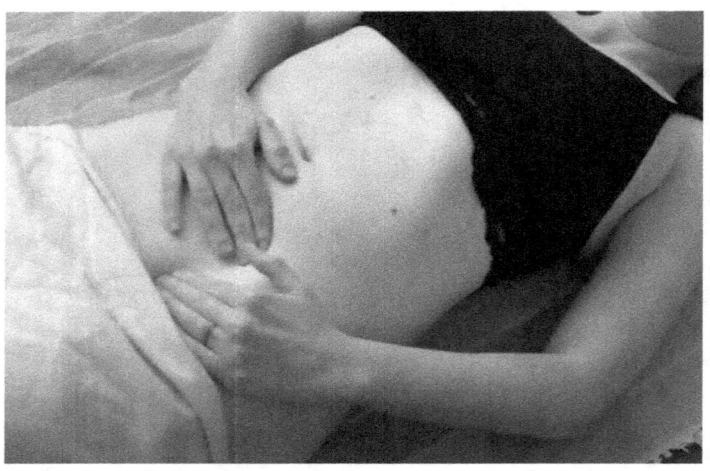

Image stills of scar tissue bodywork techniques. Source: Author.

You can do these techniques 2-3 times per week to start. As the tissue softens and sensation returns, you'll know the massage is working and can do it less frequently. Check in regularly with the following:

- Appearance: Does the scar appear more even or flat?
- Tone: How does it feel underneath—alive, soft, elastic?
- Feel: How much movement do you feel within the tissue? Does one side feel like the tissue is being pulled? Is it raised or rough?
- Sensation: Are there temperature differences along the scar? Is there numbness? Pain?

Scar Tissue Massage Routine

This routine is best done after the general abdominal and womb massage, when the tissue is already warm and receptive. At first, you may want to follow along with the video until you feel comfortable practicing on your own.

Before beginning, wipe off any oil from the skin, or use a cloth or sheet to improve traction. The pressure used should be quite deep and uncomfortable at times, but never sharp or painful.

Begin by placing your hands over your scar. Breathe deeply and attune to the sensations in this space.

Exploration + Assessment:

Trace the scar, noticing how it feels—not only along the scar itself but in the surrounding tissue as well. Stretch the tissue in all directions along the length of the scar: downward, upward, left, and right, observing how much movement is available.

Technique #1:

Apply slow, deep friction along the length of the scar, moving in a zig-zag pattern.

Technique #2:

Use a slow and deep wave-like motion along the scar.

Technique #3:

Lift the scar tissue, using a pinching motion, and roll it between your fingers along the length of the scar.

Technique #4:

Create deep, fast vibration along the length of the scar to further awaken circulation and release tension.

To close, return your hands to rest over the scar. Breathe, reconnect, and notice: Has the tissue softened? Is there more warmth, energy, or movement now?

May your healing hands bring life back into every part of you, remembering your body's innate blueprint of health.

Closing the Birth Portal

Pregnancy and birth create a profound physical and energetic opening. You may feel more tender and expanded than ever before.

The months after birth are a time of coming back together: integrating what you've lived through and rooting into a new version of yourself. Ideally, this happens within the container of community, yet even alone, it's a powerful time.

When women don't consciously seal their energy centers sometime after birth, they may remain overly open, in states of deep vulnerability or ungroundedness. While it's beautiful to be receptive, staying too open can make it difficult to root and find strength.

Nearly every traditional culture has some version of a postpartum closing ritual. The most well-known is the "closing of the bones" ceremony from Mexican tradition, where scarves or rebozos are wrapped around the mother's hips and abdomen in a loving and intentional way.

These ceremonies mark the completion of the childbearing journey and the beginning of a new chapter. They're acts of physical, emotional, and spiritual integration. Through them, you're woven anew.

The ritual that follows isn't a "closing of the bones ceremony," as that is not from my tradition, and it requires community. This is a meditation you can do on your own, or even better, with your sleeping baby on your chest.

Closing the Birth Portal Ritual

To begin, come into stillness. Place your hands on your baby, or your womb, grounding your awareness in the body. Notice any sensations, images, or feelings that come up.

Visualize the unique opening that exists in your pelvic area, the one created by your birth. Travel down to the cervix and yoni. See the ligaments that hold your pelvis together. Connect to all these open areas and then begin to see them closing and coming back together. Picture an open flower slowly coming back into a bud. Feel yourself becoming more secure, held, rooted.

Offer gratitude for the complete opening that birth required, and for the sacred work your body did. This level of openness is no longer needed.

Now, sense a new opening instead: a shimmering golden cord between your heart and your baby's heart, connecting the two of you with love.

Allow space to mourn what has passed—your maiden self, the birth experience you hoped for, or the overwhelm of new motherhood.

Call in an intention and prayer for your motherhood and this new season. Close out this ritual with gratitude.

As you close the birth portal and move into a more grounded rhythm, a new life begins.

A Healing Story

After going through a miscarriage with her first pregnancy, a woman came to me for healing support. She worked with releasing grief, a pelvic steaming practice, and sending love and compassion to her womb during massage. In an energy healing session, we both felt the image of a graveyard when contacting her womb. It still remained a living altar to her baby. She then received her soul healing symbol: rose petals. She visualized herself scattering rose petals all around the altar of her womb, moving it from a shrine of grief to something lighter and more reverent going forward.

Vitality in Motherhood

Vitality is something you source from many places: food, herbs, relationships, nature, and how you care for yourself.

It all begins with nourishment. Food is the foundation of physical vitality, allowing you to feel resourced enough to live well and make changes as needed. It helps rebuild your nutrient reserves, so you can function and think clearly. As you feel more nourished, you may find you have more resilience against stress and can show up better for others.

Nourishment is anything that is life-giving. For most of history, mothers raised children within intergenerational communities. We all lived among people we knew our whole lives and were rarely alone. Mothers co-regulated with other adults, children played freely together, and there was time for leisure and creativity.

Modern mothering, in contrast, is often isolating, which creates chronic hypervigilance and depletion that affects women, body and spirit. Having others show up for you is a balm to the human heart.

Community can be created wherever you are. It can look like staying put, showing up for friends, learning to receive, prioritizing resolving conflicts, and welcoming even imperfect connections.

Getting into nature daily is also crucial to your vitality. It supports roots chakra and pelvic health. It helps you source energy from the Earth, calms your nervous system, and regulates the biorhythms of your whole family. This happens most powerfully in wild spaces, but simply being outside makes a difference.

The nervous system affects pelvic floor health, hormone function, digestion, and overall energy. Being in nature helps restore that balance.

Prioritizing being outside more throughout the day awakens creativity and allows the attention to shift from you as the entertainer, to nature itself. Fresh air, sunshine on your skin, and the earth beneath your feet are simple, powerful medicines. Health and vitality can be so simple.

And since alone time is often rare in early motherhood, you can weave simple rituals of vitality and nourishment into your days. This supports both you and your children. You can cook meals and make herbal remedies with little helping hands. Run ritual baths and soak with them. Massage your own body and let them see how you take care of yourself.

Mothers are children's first spiritual teachers. Their life and path are their own, but mothers form the foundation of their deep belief systems (of course, they can later work on unraveling).

At my mother-line altar, I share with my daughters the women in our family. I teach them about things that are sacred and how we honor them. How we gather strength here.

Our children learn about what is sacred, what a soul-filled life looks like, how things move us, and how we move them through us.

There are so many ways to bring ritual and self-care into everyday life without needing to carve out long hours alone. Seeking this balance is important. Still, some solitude is essential; you must carve out time for something that nourishes you.

Postpartum changes you, reweaving who you are each time. Within this openness is an opportunity to feel more whole and vibrant than ever before.

Closing Blessing

May our grandmothers watch over us.

May we remember that we were once

the deepest prayer in their hearts.

May we live long enough

To watch our daughter's daughters

Become wild and wise women.

9

Integration

Reclamation and Returning Home

From first to last breaths,

Mother to daughter,

Womb to womb,

We are connected by a red thread that spans the cosmos.

BETHANY WILDE

Healing and reconnection are a spiral path. It calls you to work on and prioritize different things, in different seasons of your life. Sometimes, you embark on a soul retrieval, where healing is the sole focus. Other times, you may focus on weaving pelvic wellness or nourishment into the background of your life.

This book and the practices are all invitations. They provide you with a set of tools and practices when needed but are never required to attain vibrancy. You don't need hours of meditation or ritual to connect. Simply weaving consciousness into your daily life is the integration. This creates a different presence in your body and relationships, and awareness always shifts energy.

Live aligned with your own cyclical rhythms. What's most important is maintaining a consistent presence in your body, and a connection with your intuition to guide you. Any of the practices are simply ways to create space for seasonal or intentional deeper connection.

Reflect on everything you've learned. What information or practice changed you the most? Has anything changed how you feel in your body? Is there a particular meditation or practice you are inspired to bring into your regular life?

Living from Your Center

Moving from disconnection to rooted presence through all the perspective-shifting invitations here, as well as the practical exercises, is the work. Awakening the deep wisdom that lives within your center is the foundation of this book.

From there, you will listen to your intuition and instincts to guide you, which naturally seeks pleasure, love, and goodness.

Awakening presence especially in the pelvic bowl, which is the seat of your power, changes everything in your life: your relationships, creativity, sensuality, motherhood, and your spirituality. You don't need to *do* anything to maintain this. Simply living from your heart is living from womb wisdom. Honoring all that lives within you: emotions, stories, your power. Walking the path of the embodied, untamed woman. The exercises are pathways to deeper connection, but you truly do have everything you need within. Healing and vitality should be easeful and feel good.

One simple way to maintain a daily connection is by putting both hands over your womb while lying down before bed. Bring breath and ground your awareness within this space.

Different times of life may call for more intentional practices. When you're in deeper seasons of healing, then this book will be there for you to reference.

Golden Light Energy Clearing Ritual

This is a helpful meditation that can be done monthly or with the seasons to clear and restore your body.

Begin by lying down in a comfortable and warm place. Put both hands over your womb, or one hand on your heart while the other is on your womb.

Spend a few minutes deepening your breath and getting into a quiet, conscious, and meditative space.

Visualize now that there is a waterfall of healing and pure, golden shining light above your head. Imagine it slowly dripping down each part of your body. Clearing, healing, and rejuvenating everything in its path.

Really take your time with this visualization and spend extra attention on areas that feel resistant or like there is a lack of energy flow.

As you go through your entire body, imagine the honey-dripping golden light coming out of your feet and into the Earth, taking with it all your unwanted energies and returning it back to the cycle of life.

Collective Reclamation

Pelvic awakening is part of the collective female and planetary healing. Women's pelvic bowls mirror the wounding towards the feminine, reflecting a culture that is unwell. Many women feel disconnection, numbness, and shame within their most sacred areas. Others experience reproductive illness and pelvic floor dysfunction.

This book certainly does not have all the answers, but it's my hope that everything within serves you by offering practices and invitations for reflection and reconnection. Attuning to your emotional body and awakening sensation will only serve you in your vibrancy and well-being.

You have stores of ancient wisdom, primal energies, and universal love that are just waiting to be tapped into. You only need to quiet your heart long enough to remember this truth. Let your pelvic bowl become your anchor, a place you return to again and again.

A woman meets her power when she listens to her womb.

You've walked a spiral path in this book. May these words and practices stay with you, ready to return as needed. As we close, receive this blessing as a prayer for your path ahead.

Pelvic Bowl Blessing

May you remember your body as a holy sanctuary.

May it hold your sacred stories, your power, your great love.

May you carry the strength

and prayers of your grandmothers,

alive in the portal of your womb.

May you live long enough to be a wild, wise elder.

May you walk this Earth in beauty,

peace, blessings,

and deep, deep remembrance.

Share the Medicine

If this book resonated with you, consider leaving a review on Amazon. It helps other women find Pelvic Awakening, and even a few heartfelt sentences make a difference.

You can also share the book with a friend or post a photo or reflection on social media. Use the hashtag #pelvicawakeningbook. I love seeing how this work reaches you.

Your support helps this vision grow. Thank you for helping bring this medicine to more women.

With gratitude,

Bethany

Acknowledgements

Writing a book is like pregnancy and birth. It takes a monumental amount of energy, but the rewards are soul-fulfilling. And you never really do it alone. You receive both human and otherworldly support.

Thank you to all the early readers that helped shape the book into what it became.

My daughters: my oldest, the girl who made me a mother. It has been the great joy of my life to know you and see you become fully yourself. I can't wait to be there for all your blossoming. And this version of the book could only have happened after giving birth to my second girl. Thank you, my sweetheart, your birth was healing, redemptive, perfect.

Thank you to the elders and teachers I've learned from, that have given me a foundation and woven with my own wisdom: Leslie Stager, Sister MorningStar, Lynn Schulte, Rosita Arvigo and her teachers, among many others. The many wise women I learned from in the numerous books I've read over the years. Seren and Azra Bertrand's Womb Awakening is among the most beloved.

Thank you to all the women who have come to me seeking healing, with open hearts. Who have shared their stories, have trusted me at the holy altar of their womb. Thank you for teaching me.

And finally, the otherworldly support. I thank my mother and grandmothers for my life, and their continued halo of protection and *soul*: Laurel, Debbie, Lillian, Annie, Mollie... and all the wise, strong women who came before, whose spirit and love weave into my blood but whose names are lost, I feel you.

Citations

Introduction

1. Lochtefeld, James G. *The Illustrated Encyclopedia of Hinduism*. Rosen Pub Group, 2002.

Chapter One

1. Eisler, Riane. *Sacred Pleasure: Sex, Myth, and the Politics of the Body – New Paths to Power and Love*. Harper One, 1996.
2. Gimbutas, Marija. *The Language of the Goddess: Unearthing the Hidden Symbols of Western Civilization*. Harper San Francisco, 1991.
3. Mellart, James. *Catal Huyuk: A Neolithic Town in Anatolia*. Thames and Hudson, 1967.
4. Noble, Vicki. *Shakti Woman: Feeling Our Fire, Healing Our World*. Harper San Francisco, 1991.

5. Kvilhaug, Maria. "Defense of Marija Gimbutas' Thesis about Old Europe." *Modern Matriarchal Studies*, www.mmstudies.com/scholars/gimbutas-defense.

6. Awan, Arshad. "Intricate Beauty of Indus Valley's Mother Goddess." *The Express Tribune*, www.tribune.com.pk/story/2422370/intricate-beauty-of-indus-valleys-mother-goddess

7. (See 4)

8. "Asherah." *Wikipedia*, Wikimedia Foundation, www.en.wikipedia.org/wiki/Asherah.

9. Long, Asphodel. "The Goddess in Judaism – An Historical Perspective." *Asphodel Long*, www.asphodel-long.com/goddess-writings/the-goddess-in-judaism-an-historical-perspective.

Chapter Two

1. Stross, Brian. "The Mesoamerican Sacrum Bone: Doorway to the Otherworld." *The University of Texas at Austin*, www.research.famsi.org/aztlan/uploads/papers/stross-sacrum.pdf.

2. Maciocia, Giovanni. *The Foundations of Chinese Medicine: A Comprehensive Text for Acupuncturists and Herbalists.* Elsevier Churchhill Livingstone, 2005.

3. Resource from private manual in the Arvigo ® Techniques of Maya Abdominal Therapy practitioner training guide.

4. Silber, Sherman J. MD. "How Does the Biological Clock Work?" *The Infertility Center of St. Louis,* www.infertile.com/beating-biological.

5. Block, E. "Quantitative Morphological Investigations of the Follicular System in Women; Variations at Different Ages." *Acta anatomica,* vol. 14, 1952, doi:10.1159/000140595.

6. Stein, Rob. "Scientists Create Fertile Eggs From Mouse Stem Cells." *NPR,* 4 Oct. 2012, www.npr.org/sections/health-shots/2012/10/04/162263750/scientists-create-fertile-eggs-from-mouse-stem-cells.

7. Chia, Mantak. *Sexual Reflexology: Activating the Taoist Points of Love.* Destiny Books, 2003.

8. Fuchs, A R et al. "Oxytocin receptors in nonpregnant human uterus." *The Journal of Clinical Endocrinology*

and Metabolism, vol. 60, 1985, doi:10.1210/jcem-60-1-37.

9. Romm, Aviva MD. "Everything You Need to Know About the Pap Test, HPV, and Pelvic Exams." *Aviva Romm*, www.avivaromm.com/pelvic-exams.

10. Wolf, Naomi. *Vagina: A New Biography*. Ecco, 2013.

11. O'Connell, Helen E et al. "Anatomy of the clitoris." *The Journal of Urology*, vol. 174, 2005, doi:10.1097/01.ju.0000173639.38898.cd.

12. Pappas, Stephanie. "Nipples 'Light Up' Brain the Way Genitals Do." *LiveScience*, www.livescience.com/15380-nipples-genitals-brain-map.html.

Chapter Three

1. Dale, Cindi. *The Subtle Body: An Encyclopedia of Your Energetic Anatomy*. Sounds True, 2009.

2. Barber, Victoria. "What is Tantra?" *The British Museum.*, www.britishmuseum.org/blog/what-tantra.

Chapter Five

1. Van Der Kolk, Bessel. The Body Keeps the Score: Brain, Mind and Body in the Healing of Trauma. Penguin Books, 2014.

Chapter Six

1. Arvigo, Rosita, and Nadine Epstein. *Sastun: My Apprenticeship with a Maya Healer*. HarperOne, 1995.
2. Garza, Keli. "Research." *Steamy Chick*, www.steamychick.com/research.
3. James, Mary ND. "Topical Use of Castor Oil." *Naturopathic Doctor News & Review*, www.ndnr.com/dermatology/topical-use-of-castor-oil.

Chapter Eight

1. Sze, Eddie H. M., Gordon B. Sherard III, and Jeanette M. Dolezal. "Pregnancy, Labor, Delivery, and Pelvic Organ Prolapse." *Obstetrics & Gynecology*, vol. 100, no. 5, pt. 1, Nov. 2002, pp. 981–986. doi:10.1016/S0029-7844(02)02246-9.

2. "More Than 3.6 Million Births Recorded in the United States in 2024, Up 1 Percent From 2023." *Physician's Weekly*, 24 Apr. 2025, www.physiciansweekly.com/more-than-3-6-million-births-recorded-in-the-united-states-in-2024-up-1-percent-from-2023.

3. "Reasons for Cesarean Birth in the U.S." *Statista*, 2023, www.statista.com/statistics/1448748/reasons-for-cesarean-birth-us.

Resources

Holistic Practitioners

- The Arvigo ® Techniques of Maya Abdominal Therapy: www.arvigotherapy.com
- Institute for Birth Healing: www.instituteforbirthhealing.com/business-directory
- STRAIT Scar Tissue Release: www.marjoriebrookseminars.com/resources
- Somatic Experiencing: www.directory.traumahealing.org
- EMDR Therapy: www.emdria.org
- Birth Story Integration: www.healingbirth.net
- Somatic Vaginal Steaming Guidance + Herb Shop: www.wholesome-haven.com

Recommended Books

Female Pelvis

- The *Jade Egg: Dynamic Pelvic Floor Exercises and Vaginal Weightlifting* by Lara Eardley
- The *Female Pelvis Anatomy and Exercises* by Blandine Calais-Germain
- *The Pelvic Floor* by Beate Carrière
- *Vagina* by Naomi Wolf

Women's Wisdom

- *Everything Below the Waist: Why Healthcare Needs a Feminist Revolution* by Jennifer Block
- *Sacred Pleasure: Sex, Myth, and the Politics of the Body – New Paths to Power and Love* by Riane Eisler
- *Taking Charge of Your Fertility: The Definitive Guide to Natural Birth Control, Pregnancy Achievement, and Reproductive Health* by Toni Weschler
- *Womb Awakening: Initiatory Wisdom from the Creatrix of All Life* by Seren and Azra Bertrand

- *Women Who Run with the Wolves: Myths and Stories of the Wild Woman Archetype* by Clarissa Pinkola Estes

Childbearing Year

- *Diastasis Recti: The Whole-Body Solution to Abdominal Weakness and Separation* by Katy Bowman
- *Fertile: Prepare Your Body, Mind, and Spirit for Conception and Pregnancy to Create a Conscious Child* by Pritam Atma
- *Healing Your Body Naturally After Childbirth* by Jolene Brighten, ND
- *Preparing for a Gentle Birth: The Pelvis in Pregnancy* by Blandine Calais-Germain
- *The Fourth Trimester: A Postpartum Guide to Healing Your Body, Balancing Your Emotions, and Restoring Your Vitality* by Kimberly Ann Johnson

Deeper Healing

- *Call of the Wild: How We Heal Trauma, Awaken Our Own Power, and Use it For Good* by Kimberly Ann Johnson
- *Heal Pelvic Pain* by Amy Stein

- *Hormone Intelligence: The Complete Guide to Calming Hormone Chaos and Restoring Your Body's Natural Blueprint for Well-Being* by Aviva Romm, MD
- *Period Repair Manual: Natural Treatments for Better Hormones and Better Periods* by Lara Briden, ND
- *The Courage to Heal: A Guide for Women Survivors of Child Sexual Abuse* by Ellen Bass and Laura Davis

Energetics

- *Emergence of the Sensual Woman: Awakening Our Erotic Innocence* by Saida Desilets
- *Energetic Boundaries: How to Stay Protected and Connected in Work, Love, and Life* by Cyndi Dale
- *Sexual Awakening for Women: A Tantric Workbook* by Shakti Malan
- *Tao Tantric Arts for Women: Cultivating Sexual Energy, Love, and Spirit* by Minke de Vos
- *The Subtle Body: An Encyclopedia of Your Energetic Anatomy* by Cyndi Dale
- *Yoni Massage: Awakening Female Sexual Energy* by Michaela Riedl

Pelvic Awakening Bonus

As a gift with this book, you'll receive access to a guided abdominal and womb massage video, a foundational practice best learned through demonstration.

To access this free offering, visit:

www.pelvicawakeningbook.com

You'll be asked to enter your e-mail to receive access to the private video page.

For those wanting to go deeper, the Pelvic Awakening Sacred Practice Bundle is available as an optional upgrade. It includes additional guided videos and audio meditations to further support your healing, including scar tissue massage, castor oil packs, pelvic anatomy, breathwork, and more.

These videos are here to support your embodiment and deepen your journey of connection and healing.

About the Author

Bethany Wilde is an author, mother, and herbalist.

She spent has years working one-on-one with women as a womb and pelvic bodyworker before starting Rooted Woman Botanicals, an herbal shop offering remedies to nourish female vitality and support mothers through every season of life.

Her work weaves together embodiment, ancestral remembering, and sacred healing into words and medicine that speak to the deep intelligence of the body.

To connect with her offerings, visit:

www.rootedwomanwellness.com

For bonus practices from the book, visit:

www.pelvicawakeningbook.com

www.ingramcontent.com/pod-product-compliance
Lightning Source LLC
Chambersburg PA
CBHW062052280426
43661CB00088B/772